# Fur Coat and No Knicke

## A Comedy

Mike Harding

*Samuel French—London*
*New York – Sydney – Toronto – Hollywood*

## FUR COAT AND NO KNICKERS

First presented at the Coliseum Theatre, Oldham on the 13th September, 1980, with the following cast of characters:

| | |
|---|---|
| **Edith Ollerenshawe** <br> **Barmaid** at *The Friendship* | Judith Barker |
| **Harry Ollerenshawe** | Ted Morris |
| **Kevin Ollerenshawe** | Jeffrey Longmore |
| **Deirdre Ollerenshawe** <br> **Evette** | Diane Whitley |
| **Peter Ollerenshawe** | Andrew Hay |
| **Nip (George Albert)** | David Ross |
| **Muriel Greenhalgh** <br> **Barmaid** at *The Oddfellows* <br> **Policewoman** | Paula Tilbrook |
| **Ronald Greenhalgh** <br> **Man** in *The Catholic Club* <br> **Policeman** | Patrick Nyland |
| **Mark Greenhalgh** | Paul Gabriel |
| **Father Finbar Molloy** | Cliff Howells |
| **Hamish** | Ian Mercer |
| **Jimmy** <br> **Bouncer** <br> **Waiter** | Ian Burns |
| **Kirstene** | Kathryn Wayman |
| **Wendy** | Donna Dukes |

Directed by Kenneth Alan Taylor
Designed by Caroline McCulloch
Slide sequences by Caroline McCulloch and Stephen Selwyn

## PRODUCTION NOTES

This Acting Edition is based on the original production of the play at the Coliseum Theatre, Oldham. In that production, a revolve was used, with the sets arranged as follows:

For Act I, Scene 1, the Ollerenshawes' living-room was set on one half of the revolve, with the bar trucks required for Scenes 2–6 pre-set on the other half. In Act II, Scene 1, the Ollerenshawes' living-room was set as before, with the church for Scene 2 pre-set behind. During Scene 2, the living-room set was struck and the reception set for Scene 3.

If it is not possible to use a revolve, the sets will have to be arranged to suit the staging facilities available.

The Oldham production also used a rear-projection screen and a series of slides to illustrate the action. For example, when each character stepped downstage to speak to the audience, slides of that character were shown, and in the church, the wedding ceremony was backed up by slides of the bride, groom and guests in typical wedding poses.

## CHARACTERS

**Edith Ollerenshawe**
**Kevin Ollerenshawe,** her son
**Deirdre Ollerenshawe,** her daughter and the bride-to-be
**Harry Ollerenshawe,** her husband
**Nip (George Albert),** her father
**Peter Ollerenshawe,** her younger son
**Mark Greenhalgh,** Deirdre's fiancé
**Father Finbar Molloy,** parish priest
**Barmaid** at *The Oddfellows*
**Hamish,** the best man
**Barmaid** at *The Friendship*
**Jimmy,** Peter's friend
**Barmaid** at *The Steam Shovel*
**Man** in *The Catholic Club*
**Bouncer**
**Waiter**
**Evette,** a stripper
**Policeman**
**Policewoman**
**Kirstene**⎫
**Wendy**⎬ the bridesmaids
**Muriel Greenhalgh,** mother of the groom
**Ronald Greenhalgh,** her husband

ACT I

    Scene 1   Friday evening. The Ollerenshawes' living-room
    Scene 2   Later that evening. *The Oddfellows* Tap Room
    Scene 3   Later that evening. *The Friendship*
    Scene 4   Later that evening. *The Steam Shovel*
    Scene 5   Later that evening. *The Catholic Club*
    Scene 6   Later that evening. *The Can Can Club*

ACT II

    Scene 1   Saturday morning. The Ollerenshawes' living-room
    Scene 2   Saturday afternoon. The Church
    Scene 3   Later that afternoon. The Masonic Hall

Time—late 1970s

# ACT I

## Scene 1

*The Ollerenshawes' living-room. Friday, early evening*

*The house is on a late fifties' Northern working-class housing estate. The living-room has a cream tiled fireplace with an electric coal-effect fire in it, surrounded by a settee and armchair in black vinyl with red cushions, and a pouffe. The mantelpiece is full of little brass windmills, brass boots, nut-crackers shaped like bluebottles etc. There is a teak veneer dining-table and six chairs, with a sideboard to match. On the sideboard there are photos of children, weddings, etc., and a large one of the Pope. Dominating the far corner is a gold quilted vinyl bar with a glass top, decorated with bullfight posters, plastic onions, straw-covered bottles and a soda syphon covered with a knitted poodle. On the wall hang pictures of the Queen and the Sacred Heart. The picture of the Sacred Heart has an electric candle beneath it, which flickers when lit. There is a television DR by the fireplace*

*When the* CURTAIN *rises, the room is in semi-darkness*

*Edith Ollerenshawe enters, carrying her shopping bag. She switches on the light. The light below the Sacred Heart lights up as well. She puts down her shopping bag and straightens her back, then goes to the mantelpiece, takes a cigarette out of the packet there and lights it. She gives a puff of relief and flops on to the settee, kicking her shoes off and waggling her toes. She reaches down and rubs her calves*

**Edith** Oooh me bloody veins—they're sticking out like pea-pods. (*She wriggles her toes then stands and throws off her work-day coat*) I'll make a cup of tea before the blackface tribe come chargin' through that door.

*Edith goes off* L *to the kitchen, singing "The Rose of Tralee", la-la-ing half the words. She reappears with a mug of tea, switches on the radio and sits down*

*A typical commercial radio voice, sounding as though it comes from somewhere between Birmingham, Croydon and Connecticut, speaks on the radio*

**DJ's Voice** And now on fabulous Radio Gibberdilly it's ding-dong the bells are going to chime-time for all those lucky lasses who are getting married tomorrow. First under starter's orders, Deirdre Ollerenshawe who gets married to Mark Greenhalgh at St Thomas Parish Church, Grimesdale——

*Edith nearly drops cork-legged when she hears this*

—at twelve noon tomorrow morning. She wants to thank all the girls at Farley, Carter and Pickles where she works for all the lovely pressies and a special thanks to her mum, Edith Ollerenshawe, for all she's done for her. Here's (*singer's name*) singing *The Wedding.*

*As the music plays, Edith, in a half daze, walks over to the radio and listens in a dreamy fashion before switching it off*

**Edith**  Ooooh, it's made me feel all funny that, hearing me name on the radio, Edith Ollerenshawe, Edith Ollerenshawe. (*She moves downstage to address the audience, changing her tone*)

*The Lights fade to a spot on Edith*

Edith Ollerenshawe. I'm a chargehand at an umbrella works. Maureen, who works with me, says that when I've got my temper up, I've got a voice like somebody shovelling coke. Well, you've got to be a bit aggressive with my lot, or the place'd be like a pigsty. They give me a headache with all they do. Dress: In the house, blue nylon coverall and a cigarette. Outside, *Woman's Own* ladies' wear, I think C&A's is very good value myself, don't you? But I treated myself, and bought my wedding outfit from Lewis's. Religion: Priest, God, gossip and headache pills. Guilty Secret: Can't remember what happened once on a day trip to Llandudno after seventeen snowballs and a scampi in the basket with a bingo caller under the Great Orme in the moonlight, so I'm not really sure who our Peter's father is. Still, life goes on, dun't it? (*She goes back into character, moves upstage and sits down*)

*The Lights come up on the living-room, as Edith rummages through her shopping bag*

Chunky, juicy hamburgers. Nay, that'll not do. I nearly forgot it's Friday. Here these'll do. (*She reads from a packet*) "Captain Ahab's Cod Pieces—a ready-to-warm-up family dinner, ideal for TV snacks and busy mums." Two tins of instant spuds and a tin of corn. That should do them. (*She stands up, sees a newspaper lying on the settee and stuffs it under a cushion*) The way they leave stuff lying about, it's no wonder I've got grey hairs. Our Kevin's late.

*Edith exits* L *to the kitchen, taking the shopping bag with her*

*At the same time, our Kevin appears* DR. *The Lights fade to a spot on him*

**Kevin** (*to the audience*)  Our Kevin. That's me. Kevin Ollerenshawe, often described as a typical Jack the Lad, or as "all mouth and trousers obsessed with birds and football"—I'll go along with that. Education: Well, as far as that's concerned, I was brought up on *Star Trek, Grand-stand* and *Practical Mechanics*, which explains why I've had forty jobs since leaving school. At present I'm working in a spares department in a motor firm. Hobbies: I've only got four—birds, booze, football and cars. Dress: Always smart, finished off with gold bullion medallion and identity bracelet. Religion: I'm a Christmas Eve Roman Catholic. I regularly go to church once a year and regularly fall over a drunk at

Midnight Mass. Guilty Secret: Once kissed a bloke on a works do when I was drunk—(*he pauses*)—and I quite liked it.

*The Lights come up on the living-room*

(*Moving into the room*) Hello, anyone in?

**Edith** (*off*) Doing the tea in the kitchen.

**Kevin** It's me. Have you brewed? (*He goes over to the mantelpiece, takes a cigarette from the packet and lights it. He switches on the TV and sits down*)

*The introductory music to a children's programme comes on*

*Edith enters* L *with a mug of tea*

**Edith** (*handing him the mug of tea*) Yes, and don't you pinch any of your dad's fags off the mantelpiece. You know he'll go mad. (*Changing her tone as she takes another fag for herself*) All right, luv?

**Kevin** (*not even looking up*) What's for tea?

**Edith** Fish, new potatoes and corn.

**Kevin** Fish? Not bloody fish, I hate it.

**Edith** It's Friday.

*She exits* L *to the kitchen*

(*Off*) And watch your language in my 'ouse.

**Kevin** I know, it's Friday but we don't have to not have meat on Friday any more. The Pope said so. It's all right.

**Edith** (*off*) Well, I don't agree. It's like the mass in Latin. There's something that made it different being a Catholic and fish and Latin were two of them.

**Kevin** And drunken Irish priests and bingo are two others.

*Edith enters* L, *carrying a tray of crockery, cutlery etc.*

**Edith** (*as she enters*) What did you say?

**Kevin** I said I wonder when our Deirdre's coming home?

*Deirdre enters* DR, *wearing a coat and hat completely covered in toilet paper and ribbons. The Lights fade to a spot on her*

**Deirdre** (*to the audience*) Hey, I'm getting married tomorrow. Deirdre Ollerenshawe, by the way. Secretary to a local estate agent. Now, I'm a smart dresser, I go for tight sweaters, pencil skirts slit up to the thigh, high-heeled shoes—well, you've got to keep up with the fashion, haven't you? I am also what you might call "aspiring", well that's what it said in last month's *Cosmopolitan*. I like *Cosmo*, I think it is very educational. I also read *Woman*, oh, and I once read a copy of *Forum*—I found it on the bus—well, those sort of things don't go on, do they? Religion: Bungalows, Newquay and money. Hobbies: Buying clothes—usually from Chelsea Girl, browsing in furniture shops, and dancing. Guilty Secret: I once went all the way with a fairground lad, well, all my friends had done it. I didn't like it much anyway, it was all a bit too physical for me—I've never liked anything physical, I hated PE at school.

*The Lights come up on the living-room*

(*Moving into the room*) Hello! I'm home.

**Edith** Well, you look a duck. Ooh, they played a record for you on the radio. That nice disc jockey it was, Dusty Wilson.

**Deirdre** I know! I heard it. I had a few drinks at dinner time to celebrate with some of the girls from work and when we got back to the office we had a few sherries in the medical room and they all did this to me. They're a silly lot. (*She goes over to the mantelpiece*) Do you think I could pinch one of my dad's fags?

**Kevin** You leave 'em alone, he'll go mad if they're all gone.

**Deirdre** He won't miss one. (*She takes a cigarette and lights it*) Is Peter back yet?

**Edith** (*laying the table*) I saw him in town. He says he won't be back till half-five. He's working in the library on his book.

**Deirdre** He wants to get a proper job instead of pretending he can write. I'm ashamed to death of him I am. Mrs Greenhalgh asked me how he was getting on yesterday and I had to tell her he was working as a rep for a double-glazing firm.

**Edith** Our Deirdre!

**Kevin** What the 'ell did you tell 'er that for?

**Deirdre** (*removing her hat and coat*) It was the first thing that came into my head. I couldn't tell her he was on the dole and the last time he was asked what he did he said he was a poet and the dole clerk said there aren't any jobs for poets this week but if he could see his way to laying a few bricks at the same time as he was thinking his beautiful thoughts he might have been able to help him.

**Edith** Mother of God. What will we do if Mrs Greenhalgh finds out?

**Kevin** What're you worrying about? She won't find out and anyway, so what if she does, it's their Mark our Deirdre's marrying, not her.

**Edith** But what if she finds out it was him who wrote that article about Mr Greenhalgh and the Corporation Diesel in that paper?

**Kevin** They won't know that the pillock who signs himself Ned Ludd in the *Grimesdale Alternative Free Press and Bugle* is your out-of-work, layabout, hairy-arsed son.

**Edith** Well, I just hope not for our Deirdre's sake. (*She goes to the mantelpiece and takes another fag and then remembers that Kevin has just sworn*) And watch your language in my house. (*To Deirdre*) I've sorted the cake out, love. We pick it up half-eleven in the morning and Mrs Adam's coming round with the dress tonight like you asked and the hairdresser said if you get our Kevin to pick up the flowers at the same time as she's doin' us.

**Kevin** Me?

**Edith** Yes you. You can do something for your sister for a change.

*Deirdre exits* L *to the kitchen*

**Kevin** I don't know why we 'ave to 'ave all that fuss about gettin' wed. Why can't she live in sin. They're all doin' it now you know, it's the "in thing". William Hickey says "All the best people live over the brush". (*He gets up for another fag, lights it and sits down*)

*Deirdre enters* L *with a mug of tea*

**Deirdre** What did he say?

**Edith** I'll wash your mouth out with soap, you rotten little devil. You're not too big, you know, me lad, so you needn't be so clever. (*She clouts him on the back of the head*)

**Deirdre** (*lapsing into dialect as she does when angry*) I'm not like that, our Kevin. I think more about meself than them scrubbers you knock about with.

**Kevin** Like who?

**Deirdre** Like that Carol Dugdale. She's been with every lad in the town that'll have 'er, she 'as. She can't walk properly 'cos she's that used to being on her back, she gets dizzy when she stands up.

**Edith** Our Deirdre!

**Deirdre** Well, it's true. It was her fault that Grimesdale Town got knocked out of the Rugby League First Division last season. She went with every bloke in the team the night before the match and they were all too knackered to run the next day. Hull beat 'em thirty-six to three.

**Edith** Our Deirdre, don't be so coarse!

**Deirdre** Well, it's true, Mam.

**Kevin** Anyway, how do you know I've been with her?

**Deirdre** Ellen Sayers told me she'd seen you out walkin' with your arms round her.

**Kevin** Ellen Sayers she can talk. She bangs like a chip-shop door, she does.

**Edith** Our Kevin!!! (*She takes another fag*)

*A door slams, off*

Here's your father, you'd better not let him hear you talking like that either of you.

*They all look off* R

*Harry Ollerenshawe enters* R, *dressed in full motor-cycle kit. He is wearing his helmet, but one boot is off. He shouts something with his visor down, but no-one can hear him*

**Kevin** We can't hear you.

*Harry opens his visor and points down at his foot*

**Harry** Next door's dog has crapped on our path again—I've a good mind to make him next door clean my boot up.

**Edith** How do you know it was next door's dog?

**Harry** It's always in the same spot.

**Kevin** Then why do you tread in it? You should know where it is by now.

**Harry** Me bloody visor was steamed up! (*He starts to take off his gear and is, of course, half the size with it all off. He mutters as he takes the stuff* *off*) Shouldn't be allowed to keep dogs them sort. It eats better than me, that bloody dog.

*Everyone ignores him as he speaks—Deirdre continues laying the table, Kevin watches TV*

*Edith exits L to the kitchen*

A pound of steak a day it gets. They're mental defectives that lot. Him and his Jehovah's Witnesses. I'd do what Hitler did with them, I would. Bangin' on everybody's door like that. Salesmen, that's all they are, selling false religions. They should burn 'em.

*Edith enters L with a mug of tea, which she hands to Harry*

(*Picking up the now empty cigarette packet from the mantelpiece*) Who's smoked all me bloody fags?

*Edith exits L to the kitchen*

**Deirdre** Not me, I've got me own.
**Kevin** I don't smoke tipped.
**Edith** (*off*) I borrowed one, love.
**Harry** You can't leave anything down in this house without someone pinches it. If it isn't you lot, it's that robbin' old bugger of a father of yours. I suppose he's coming for his tea, is he?

*Nip enters DR, wearing a flat cap and only one shoe. The Lights fade to a spot on him as he says his piece*

**Nip** (*to the audience*) How do? Now then, I'm George Albert, known to my friends as "Nip", Edith Ollerenshawe's father. I suppose you might describe me as "going a bit deaf but not daft". I'm still working, though I should have retired long ago, for a dairy farmer at Moorend. When I'm not working I'm in t' pub. I like a drink, and when I've had a few, I fancy t'women an' all. I'm a rum bugger tha knows. I have what you might call a "ripe" vocabulary—bollocks! Hobbies: Playing dominoes, work and women. Religion: *Oddfellows, T'Brown Cow* and *T'Friendship*. I regularly get banned from *T'Friendship* for pouring beer in t' juke-box and fusing it. Bloody modern music, gets on your wick. It's all bang-bang and shoutin'. Guilty Secrets: Well, you don't reach my age and not have a few secrets, but I don't feel guilty about any of them. They were all free, white and over twenty-one. Well, over twenty-one anyway.

*The Lights come up on the living-room, as Nip moves into the room*

'Lo Kevin, Harry, Deirdre, where's your mam? 'Ave you gorra dog? I've just trod in summat.
**Edith** (*off*) I'm in the kitchen, Dad, getting the tea.
**Nip** I'll just come and give you a hand, love.

*Nip exits L to the kitchen*

**Harry** "Give you a hand, love." Ay, his hand in her purse. He's gone to

cadge a fiver off her, the old bugger. Should be put down when they get
that bloody age. Hitler had the right idea. Burn the buggers when they
get senile like that. (*Shouting to Edith off* L) Did anything come for me
from *Motor-cycle News*?

**Edith** (*off*) There's a packet for you on the telly.

**Harry** About time too. They must have sent it via bloody Australia. (*He
picks up the packet from the TV and reads the address label*) "Mr Harold
Ollerenshawe." (*He moves downstage*)

*The Lights fade to a spot on Harry*

(*To the audience*) I'm a foreman at the sole-cutting machine shop at
the slipper works—the Pussyfoot. I'm proud to be British and I don't
give a bugger who knows it. I fought in North Africa—with Monty—I
bled for you lot—and when I look around me I wonder why I bothered.
I helped to defeat Hitler, but I must say I admire the way he ran his
country—with discipline and order. Two things that are sadly lacking
in this country today. I was educated at Catterick camp, the Pioneer
Corps and Waddi Ben Aboun Naafi. Dress: As a man of authority at a
slipper works should do. Hobbies: The motor bike first, and the mysteries
of the Catholic Church and Littlewoods eight-draw system second.
Religion: I'm an ardent Roman Catholic. Guilty Secret: I—er—once
had a quick knee-tremble with the forelady of the furry pom-pom store.
Went to confession right away though, got ten Hail Marys, ten Our
Fathers and seventeen Glory Bes to run consecutively.

*The Lights come up on the living-room*

*Edith enters* L, *carrying a tray with five plates of food. Nip follows her with
the teapot, which he puts on the table*

**Edith** (*as she puts the plates on the table*) Here it is—our Peter's is in the
oven for when he gets in.

**Harry** (*going back into character and moving upstage*) Where's he, then, the
bloody Charles Dickens of Grimesdale?

**Edith** He's at the library working on his book.

**Harry** Book. (*Snorting*) Bloody books. That's a laugh. The day he gets
one printed I'll show me bum on Hardcastle Crags.

**Edith** You watch your language in my house and come and get your tea.
It's no wonder I'm going grey.

*They all sit down at the table to eat*

**Deirdre** (*to Edith*) Have you had a good day, Mother?

**Edith** Ooh! We had terrible trouble in work today. You know Maureen,
the girl who works for Mr Grayson. Well, she had an hour off to go to
the doctor's this morning because she's been having terrible trouble
passing her motions.

**Deirdre** Not when we're having tea, Mother.

**Edith** Well, she hasn't been really regular for months. Sometimes she can't
go for a week and a half and then when she does she says it nearly

makes her cross-eyed. Well, she's tried everything—the bran, dates and drinking a lot—she drinks like a fish anyway. Anyway, the doctor examined her and upset her to begin with when he asked her if her stools were a funny colour and she said the scouts had painted them for bob-a-job week. She thought he meant the ones in the kitchen. So there was a right mix-up about that. Then he asks her had she any trouble with her back passage before, and she said the window cleaner left his bike there once and the kids let his tyres down. So he examines her and tells her she's got a plastic colon caused by her nerves bein' upset on account of her husband and her having a bit of trouble.

**Kevin** It's a *spastic* colon.

**Edith** Oh ay! Anyway, she leaves the doctor's and goes home on her way back to the office to get her dinner hour finished. And when she goes in, she finds her husband, who should be out on his pop round, standing in the bedroom lookin' at himself in the mirror wearing her panties, bra, suspenders, fish-net stockings, the lot.

**Nip** Bloody 'ell fire!

**Edith** Well, she asked him what the hell he thought he was doing and he said he came home to get changed when he spilt a load of Dandelion and Burdock down himself and he put her clothes on by mistake. Of course, she didn't believe him because she said she'd wondered why a lot of her knickers and things had seemed slack on her recently—'cos he weighs sixteen and a half stones, her husband, he used to be a wrestler. So she walked out on him and came back to work, and she was in an awful state.

**Deirdre** Who wouldn't be?

**Edith** And we could tell that something was wrong because instead of answering "The Kismet Parasol Company" on the phone like she usually did, she said "The Kismy Arasol Company".

**Deirdre** Oooh, Mother.

**Edith** Then she screamed an obscenity down the phone and threw her coffee all over the duplicator and when Mr Roberts, my boss, asked her what was wrong, she just said "Men, you're all bent. I suppose you'd like to get into my knickers too"—just as Mrs Roberts walked in to get the car keys to pick up the kids from school. Well, that took some sorting out but Mrs Eldon did it by sitting her down and giving her some aspirins and a gin and hot water. They let her come home early.

**Deirdre** Well, I always said this was a common estate.

**Harry** What the 'ell does a grown man get out of dressing up as a woman? Tell me that. I know what I'd do with 'em. I'd do what Hitler did I would. Going round like tarts doin' it to each other. I'd burn 'em I would. When we were in the Army in North Africa . . .

**Kevin** I tell you what. I'd have liked to have seen him in them fish-net stockings—must have looked like sixteen and a half stone of steam pudding in a keepnet. Do you never fancy doing anything like that, Dad?

**Harry** Like what?

**Kevin** Gettin' dressed up in me mam's gear. I could just see you going

down the Buffs in them Aertex passion-killers and them suits of armour she beats to death in the sink every week.
**Harry** You can get knotted, you can.
**Deirdre** Ooh, you are common, our Kevin. You've a mouth like a corporation tip.
**Edith** Well, it's all right, he'll be sorry. They never do well his sort—it'll be another death-bed repentance.
**Kevin** Who's she talkin' about, me—me dad or the bloke in the kecks and the Trueform bra?
**Edith** You, and don't you use language like that in my house.
**Kevin** Like what?
**Edith** Like you know what.
**Kevin** 'Ow can I know what till you tell me what.
**Deirdre** Grow up will you, our Kevin.
**Kevin** Me—grow up! Listen to her. She thought cunilingus was a clever Irish airline until she discovered Smirnoff.
**Deirdre** (*near to tears*) Mother, did you 'ear that?
**Nip** (*ignoring them all*) What's for pudding?
**Edith** (*not having really heard what Kevin said*)) Birds Eye jam roly-poly and shut-up our Kevin and you—(*pointing at Deirdre*)—come and give me a hand and have less to say—you're not a married woman in your own house yet.

*Deirdre helps Edith to collect the dirty plates on to the tray, and exits L to the kitchen*

(*As she goes*) You'll give me all a headache you will yet. I can feel one of me 'eads comin' on.

*Edith exits L to the kitchen*

**Harry** Where's bloody Longfellow then?
**Kevin** Our Peter?
**Harry** Ay.
**Kevin** He'll be here soon I suppose. Friday's his day for doing his article for the *Grimesdale Alternative Free Press and Bugle*. He'll have been snooping round all afternoon trying to find out which councillor's been looking under the gents' lavatory door in Piecemarket Square and what happened to the money for the new slide for the kids' playing fields and why Councillor Greenhalgh's expense account included a trip to Switzerland to look at the possibility of turning Grimesdale into a plastic ski resort with alpine lanterns in Gartside Street and *après-ski* in *The Bargee and Ferret*. Such stuff can topple governments.
**Harry** He's bloody puddled, our Peter.

*Peter enters DR with his shoe in his hand. The Lights fade to a spot on him*

**Peter** (*to the audience*) Peter Ollerenshawe. Chief reporter, *Grimesdale Alternative Free Press and Bugle*. Part-time drop-out and amateur Marxist. Armchair anarchist and professional moaner. Failed university then went to teachers' training college. Left after a year. Is supposed to be writing a novel. Has had two poems printed in *Tribune*. Long hair, smokes dope. Me mother only knows about the first because I use her shower cap. Hobbies: Argument, sci-fi, head music and part-time vegetarianism. Colour Supplement/*Private Eye*/ *South Bank Show* coupled with extreme Northern Chauvinism and Oblomovitis. World revolves round pub/library/girlfriend and the major novel I am writing about the North. An amalgam of D. H. Lawrence, George Formby, Jack Kerouac and Noddy. Dress: Corduroys, Kickers, check shirt and navy-type Kerouac-style jacket. Poet on the road. Religion: Leylines, cosmic spirals, Stonehenge and earth forces. Guilty Secret: I pinch most of me ideas.

*The Lights come up on the living-room*

(*Moving into the room*) Evening. (*To Harry*) *Guten Abend mein Führer*. (*He gives a Nazi salute*) Fish, is it? That dog's done it again. (*He throws his shoe in the corner*)

**Nip** (*shouting through to the kitchen*) Our Peter's here.

**Peter** Now Grandad—all right are you? (*He turns the pictures to the wall while no-one's looking, then sits down at the table*)

**Nip** Not bad, mustn't grumble. If you do, no bugger listens.

**Harry** What time do you call this?

*Edith enters L with a plate of food*

**Edith** (*putting the plate in front of Peter*) Here's your tea, love. I kept it warm.

*Edith exits L to the kitchen*

**Peter** Thanks, Mum. (*To Harry*) It's quarter to six, *mein Kommandant*, and I've been working.

**Kevin** He's been putting Grimesdale on the map again.

**Peter** You can laugh, man, but if you knew half the things that went on in this town, you'd throw up.

**Kevin** Like what?

**Peter** Like the bent councillor and town hall officials that feather their own bloody nests, man. That's what.

**Nip** They're all bloody bent.

**Harry** Hitler had the right idea—strong government and burn the buggers.

**Kevin** So everybody's bent. It's human nature, ain't it. If you divided all the money in the world and gave it out equally it'd all be back in the same hands in a couple of years. Some people have got it and some haven't.

**Peter** And that's your excuse for doing nothing, is it? Well that's good, man. That's really good. Sit back and let the right-wing International Neo-Imperialists and Capitalists rip us off.

**Harry** The bloody unions are too strong. They don't want to work, these Trotskyites. Hitler knew what to do with Communists. They just disrupt the country. They don't support Britain. They've no pride in their country. No loyalty.

**Nip** What make's that motor bike of yours?

**Harry** Kawasaki, why? What's that got to do with it?

**Nip** Funny bloody English name that, "Kawasaki", is it Welsh?

**Peter** You're all blinded by the stuff you read in rags like the *Daily Mail*, *The Sun* and the bloody *Express*. They're all part of the establishment, man. They just control all the means of information.

**Kevin** There's a bloody good racing page in the *Express*.

**Peter** And tits and bum in *The Sun*. That's the trouble with the working class. Stick 'em on concrete estates, pay 'em nothing, rip 'em off, but as long as they've got tits and bums and racing, they're as happy as bloody lemmings on a cliff edge.

*Edith enters* L *with four plates of jam roly-poly and custard on a tray*

**Edith** (*as she enters*) How dare you use language like that before the Sacred Heart.

**Peter** I didn't know it was his turn.

*Deirdre enters* L *with another two sweet plates*

**Deirdre** You just think it's clever to blaspheme, our Peter. You think you're so high and mighty because you went to grammar school. (*She sits down*)

**Peter** Here she is—Juliet waiting breathlessly for her Romeo to claim her as his own. Heloise awaiting her Abelard. Mark Greenhalgh, he's as bright as the inside of a cow's bum.

**Deirdre** Mother, are you going to let him speak to me like that.

**Edith** You're not to talk like that about Mark, our Peter. He's a very nice boy.

**Peter** He's a pillock.

*Mark appears* DR. *The Lights fade to a spot on him as he does his bit to the audience*

**Mark** Mark Greenhalgh. As bright as the inside of a cow's bum. I work in my father's garage and road haulage business as a "director". I'm as thick as two short planks, but I'm good-looking and rich. I drive a Jensen and go power-boat racing on the reservoirs above Grimesdale Crags. I've tried to develop a non-regional accent (*he says this with a Northern "U"*) and consider myself one of the lads when I want to be. I'm basically a pratt who uses phrases like "Course we'll have a few sprogs in a year or two and we'll need an extra room then, won't we little lady, after we've calved". Dress: Very smart casuals most of the time. Very Jaeger. Religion: C. of E. but I'm "turning" for Deirdre. Guilty Secret: I suffer from premature ejaculation—which seems to suit Deirdre.

*Mark exits* R

*The Lights come up on the living-room*

**Kevin** So you're not coming out with us on Mark's bachelor night then?

**Peter** I've got better things to do.

**Kevin** Oh, come on it'll be a laugh.

**Edith** Don't get him so drunk he's in no state for the morning.

**Kevin** That's what bachelor nights are for, Mam. Getting drunk with the lads, throwing up and all that.

**Edith** Throwing up—you're like a load of animals.

*There is a knock at the door, off*

Oooh, that'll be Father Molloy. (*Shouting*) Come in, Father! He said he'd pop round to see how we were. (*Shouting*) The door's open, Father.

*The men all get up, ready to make their escape*

**Kevin** I'm goin' to get washed and ready.

*Kevin exits R*

**Peter** Me too.

*Peter exits R*

**Harry** I'll go and put me stuff away.

*Harry exits R, taking his motor-cycle gear with him*

**Nip** I'm buggering off to the pub. I'll go the back way.

*Nip exits L*

**Deirdre** You Godless lot.

*Father Molloy enters R with one shoe on. He has a hole in his sock. He is a plump, bespectacled Irish priest and although he is incoherent at the best of times, he gets worse after a couple of drinks*

**Father Molloy** God bless all here. And how are ye all? Looking forward to tomorrow I don't doubt. I should think y'are.

**Edith** Well, I won't say it isn't something I haven't looked forward to for quite a while. Would you like a cup of tea, Father?

**Father Molloy** I wouldn't say no, I'm destroyed with the walkin'.

**Edith** (*pouring out a mug of tea*) Would you like a drop of something in it, Father? It's a cold night out. (*She takes a bottle of whisky from the bar*)

**Father Molloy** Well, that would be nice. Not too much now. Maedenagam as they say. That's Greek for "all things in moderation". Oedipus went and blinded himself because he didn't have it. Hubris he had.

**Edith** (*pouring a large measure of whisky into the tea*) That's nice. They say it's hot in Greece. Tortoises come from there don't they? (*She hands the tea to Father Molloy*)

**Father Molloy** I've told the organist to be there at a quarter to and then there'll be time to sort a few things out so to speak as it were. (*He drinks his tea in one*)

**Edith** Would you like a drop more tea, Father?

**Father Molloy** Ah that would be nice now.

*Edith pours a bit of tea and a large Scotch into his mug*

Do you know it's been a busy week for the baptisms and burials. I've so many buryin's now Mr Thompson at the cemetery says he's going to ask the Bishop for a JCB and if there are any more baptisms we'll have to sink a holy-water well.

*Edith is tidying the plates away with Deirdre, not really listening*

**Edith** That's nice. They're good them JCBs.

*As Father Molloy talks, the two women go in and out L to the kitchen as they clear the table*

**Father Molloy** (*helping himself to the whisky*) I was talkin' to the Bishop last week and he said the weddin's is up on the funerals from last year but the baptisms is down on them both. So there's a bit of miscalculatin' goin' on. I had an old soul in the confessional last week near had me fallin' off me chair laughin'.

**Edith** Ooh! Whatever happened?

**Father Molloy** Well, I'd come five minutes late to start confessions and she was in the box when I got in. Course she was in the other side and it was pitch black 'cos she hadn't found the light switch and the old soul had fallen asleep. I could hear her snorin' through the grille so I banged on the ledge and shouted "Hello!" but there was no answer so I banged again and shouted "Hello! What do you want?" and she woke up and shouted "Two bottles of Guinness and put the light on in the snug!"

*The Lights fade to a Black-out. Irish jig music (the Chieftans or the Castle Ceilidh Band) plays to cover the scene change*

*The following scenes should be sketched in quickly rather than worked on at any great length, the idea being to give a feeling of accelerating movement towards drunkenness and catastrophe. Two bar areas are set at either side of the stage to represent the various pubs, and the scenes alternate between them, finishing with the apron for the final scene*

SCENE 2

*"The Oddfellows" Tap Room*

*The Lights come up on Nip leaning on the bar with a bottle, smoking his pipe*

*The Barmaid enters and starts wiping the table. She is singing "Delilah" raucously*

**Barmaid** 'Ey, doesn't your Deirdre get married tomorrow?

**Nip** Ay, she gets wed at half-past twelve and he'll be wishin' he were dead by half-past one.

**Barmaid** Don't you agree with marriage then?

**Nip** It's all right for lunatics and them as can't look after themselves but I reckon nowt to keepin' another man's daughter.

**Barmaid** Go on, you don't mean it.

**Nip** Ah do, ah reckon gettin' married is like fancyin' cream cake and then 'avin' to eat it for the rest of your life.

**Barmaid** Now where would you be without us women. I bet you wouldn't mind a bit of young stuff given the chance.

**Nip** She'd 'ave to ask me nicely and 'ave plenty of brass. Romance is all right but brass lasts. And she'd 'ave to be on t' pill. I wouldn't want to get 'er into trouble—not for a while at least.

**Barmaid** Ee—you mucky old devil.

**Nip** Nay, you can ger a good tune out of an old banjo you know.

*Kevin, Mark and Hamish, Mark's friend from the rugby club, enter*

**Barmaid** Ay, if the strings aren't broke.

*Nip and the Barmaid laugh together at her joke*

**Kevin** 'Lo, Grandad.

**Nip** Now then Kevin, what you 'avin'?

**Kevin** No, we'll get 'em. You can't afford to buy a round of drinks.

**Nip** I weren't buying a round of drinks. I were goin' to buy you one. Who are these with you?

**Kevin** 'Ey, I forgot you 'aven't met each other, 'ave you. This is Mark, that's marryin' our Deirdre and this is—what did you say your name was?

**Hamish** Hamish.

**Nip** Amos?

**Hamish** No, Hamish.

**Nip** I'll never remember that, I'll call you Amos.

**Hamish** (*sarcastically*) Thanks a lot.

**Nip** (*not giving a toss*) You're welcome.

**Kevin** Pint of bitter for me. What's yours?

**Hamish** I'll have the same.

**Mark** I'll stick to beer for a bit.

**Kevin** And one for you, Grandad?

**Nip** Who's paying?

**Hamish** It's my round actually. What would you like, Methuselah?

**Nip** I'll 'ave a large rum with a splash of lemonade, Cherub.

*They sit down at the table*

(*To Mark*) So you're the lucky one are you?

**Mark** Yes.

**Nip** You look a bit of a bloody drip. I don't suppose I'll be troubled with any great-grandchildren for a bit.

**Kevin** Take no notice of me grandad, he's always like this with strangers at first.

*The Barmaid brings over the drinks and sets them on the table*

**Hamish** I suppose you're one of those who fought and bled in two World Wars for people like me.

**Nip** I am bloody 'ellerslike. I spent both World Wars down t'pit, in t'pub and in bed wi' anyone who'd 'ave me. (*To Hamish*) Where are you from?

**Hamish** My folks are Scots but I was born near Higginshaw.

**Nip** I 'ad a lass from Higginshaw once. You want to be careful, you might be talkin' to your father.

*Hamish looks non-plussed*

**Mark** We went water ski-ing on Higginshaw Reservoir last week.

*There is a silent pause all round*

**Nip** What brought that up?

**Mark** I just thought I'd mention it.

**Nip** What d'yer do when yer go water ski-in' then?

**Mark** You put a pair of skis on and somebody pulls you behind a speedboat.

**Nip** You must be bloody puddled to spend your brass doin' that.

**Kevin** (*trying to change the subject*) You'll know Mark's dad, Grandad.

**Nip** Who?

**Kevin** His dad, he runs that big Mercedes Garage down Bessemer Lane. Ron Greenhalgh.

**Nip** Oh him—ay. (*To Mark*) So you're Ron Greenhalgh's lad. I used to kick his arse for him for stealing off my allotment, your dad. You're 'is lad, are yer? Well, yer can afford to get me a double rum for all the bloody goosegogs your old man pinched.

*Mark gets up and goes to the bar. The Barmaid sets up another round of drinks*

Ronald Greenhalgh, didn't he marry that Muriel Lees, 'er they used to call Pearl Harbour 'cos she did more to knacker the Yanks than the Japanese.

**Kevin** Shurrup Grandad, he can hear you.

*Mark brings over the tray of drinks*

**Nip** I don't give a bugger who can hear me. (*He downs his drink in one*)

**Hamish** (*to Kevin*) He's going to make himself ill.

**Nip** Right, where are we gooin' next?

**Mark** Are you coming with us?

**Nip** Ay, if you lot's buying.

**Hamish** But we thought we'd go to a disco and a night-club—you know, strippers and all that. Tits and bums, girlies you know, totties.

*They all start to get up*

**Nip** Bloody real do! Well, I've got me membership card for Hebers Working Men's Club. If any of them are affiliated, I'll sign us in.

**Barmaid** (*tidying up after them*) You want affiliating you do, Nip.

**Kevin** Come on, sup up. (*To Mark*) It's all right. We'll gerrim plastered and drop him off somewhere.

**Nip** What?

**Kevin** Nothing. Come on.

*They all start to exit*

**Nip** I'm right right behind you said the General. Where we gooin'?

**Kevin** I said we'd 'ave one with me dad.

**Nip** Well I 'ope 'e remembers it's 'is bloody round. Ah bowt him a drink last year.

*They exit*

*The Lights fade to a Black-out*


SCENE 3

*"The Friendship"*

*The Lights come up on Harry, who is leaning on the bar talking at a bored Barmaid*

**Harry** Sittin' there 'e war with 'is trousers round his ankles a fag in 'is mouth 'an the bloomin' *New Delhi Times* or somethin' spread out on his knees. I said, "Ey Sabu, it didn't take you long to catch on to English ways, did it? You've been in 'ere an 'our and an arf". So he started jabbering on about race discrimination or summat an' I just said "Ey Sabu, me foreman, you new sweeper-upper. Pull up trousers, chop chop, grab brush and sweepy sweepy. That way you get many backsheesh on Friday. Not get backsheesh sittin in khazi readin' *New Delhi Observer*. Then the cheeky bugger tells me 'ee's a doctor working during is' summer holidays from medical school!

**Barmaid** 'Ave you got many of 'em at Pussyfoot?

**Harry** About twenty. They're all right. Some of 'em you 'ave to treat 'em like kids. Trouble is they all look the same. I made one of 'em char wallah last week. Showed 'im 'ow to work the Burco. For a few days the tea was great. Yesterday mornin' the tea was lousy, just like maiden's water. I went to him. I said "Ey, char wallah, tea no good". It turns out it weren't him it were a pal of 'is standing in for 'im while 'e helped 'is brother run 'is knickers stall on Grimesdale Market.

**Barmaid** Well I never! In't it funny what goes on?

**Harry** 'Itler was right you know. *Lebensraum* he called it—everyone in his right place. When I was in North Africa . . .

**Barmaid** Hey up, here's your mates.

*Kevin, Nip, Hamish and Mark enter*

'Ello, lads.

**Nip** A double rum with a splash of lemonade for me, 'Arry.

**Harry** Oh . . . right, 'er what you lads 'avin?

**Kevin** Large Scotch.

**Mark** Well. If we're startin' on the hard stuff, I'll have the same.

**Hamish** Me too. (*To the Barmaid*) Hello sweet, d'you live with your parents?

**Barmaid** (*turning to get the drinks*) No me husband, an' 'e bites pigs' 'eads off for 'obby.

**Kevin** Well, a slice off a cut loaf's never missed.

**Barmaid** He'll be missin' a slice off his face if he's not careful. 'Ee's a bouncer at the *Can Can Club* and he eats lads like you for supper. (*She puts the drinks on the counter*)

**Kevin** Right lads, are we sittin' down or what, my brains are 'urtin'.

*They all sit down*

**Nip** Ey, 'Arry, 'ave you seen this? (*He puts three coins on the table*) There's some coins there, 'ow many can you see?

**Harry** Three, three two-pences.

**Nip** I can see eleven.

**Harry** Can ye buggery.

**Nip** I can, I can see eleven.

**Harry** There's three there.

**Nip** You can do anythin' you like. Move 'em about, anything but I say I can show you eleven coins there.

**Harry** There's only three.

**Nip** All right, if I'm wrong will you buy me a drink?

**Harry** All right, yer on.

**Nip** Right, I'm wrong. I'll 'ave a double rum with a splash of lemonade.

**Harry** Yer what?

**Nip** I said "Will you buy me a drink if I'm wrong?" You said yes, so I'm wrong. Ger us a rum.

*Everyone laughs except Harry*

**Harry** You cheeky old bugger. (*To the Barmaid*) A double rum and a splash. Hitler war right you know, they should be put down when they get his age, senile like that.

*The Lights fade to a Black-out*


SCENE 4

"*The Steam Shovel*"

*The Lights come up on Peter in conversation with Jimmy, an earnest young man who is smoking a joint. The Barmaid is behind the bar*

**Peter** But if they knew the truth they still wouldn't do anything about it.

**Jimmy** Softened by colour telly, bingo and horse-racing.

**Peter** Convenience foods and Librium. Do you know half the women in this country are on Librium or Valium, man.

**Jimmy** (*smoking the joint*) But with everybody drugged or poisoned by the establishment and the yellow press Imperialist running dogs, it'll be easy for them to step in and take total control—incite a riot—call in the special groups and there you go man, totalitarian state—they've got closed circuit video in the Arndale Centre now.

**Peter** Ey man . . . is it cool to smoke dope in here?

**Jimmy** Sure, nobody bothers. They got busted once and got the Chief Constable's son so they never did it again.

*The gang including Harry enter. All except Nip are beginning to show signs of the wallop they've walloped. Harry is arguing with Hamish, Mark is leaning a bit on Kevin and Nip is walking with his hands in his pockets*

**Harry** (*as he enters*) You can ask anybody who fought in North Africa and they'll tell you t'same thing. Rommel was the best general of the Second World War on either side.

**Hamish** He killed himself when they lost.

**Harry** He were highly strung.

**Mark** I'm gonna get drunk, really, really really drunk.
(*Singing*) It was on the Good Ship Venus
                    By God you should 'ave seen us.

**Kevin** 'Ullo, Peter.

**Peter** You're in a right state. 'Ow many 'ave you 'ad?

**Kevin** It's me grandad. 'E challenged us all to a drinkin' match, an 'alf-pint of any spirits we fancied and 'e won.

*Kevin, Mark, Hamish and Harry sit down*

**Peter** What was the prize?

**Kevin** An 'alf-pint of any spirit 'ee fancied.

**Peter** 'Ee's supposed to 'ave a bad 'eart.

**Kevin** 'Ee's thrown all his tablets down the grid again.

**Nip** Come on, Amos, it's your round.

**Hamish** (*nearly crying*) Hamish! Hamish! I'm called bloody Hamish. My mother and father were from Ecclefechan. It's not my fault.

**Nip** All right Amos, keep your bloody 'air on ... Mine's a large rum with a splash of lemonade (*Sitting down*) Now our Peter, 'oo's this?

*Hamish goes up to the bar to get the drinks. The Barmaid sets up the drinks*

**Peter** Jimmy, a friend of mine. He works on the paper with me.

**Kevin** (*in a loud whisper*) Ey, shurrup will you, they don't know you work on the paper.

**Peter** Well, they'll find out soon enough.

**Kevin** Well, keep it quiet till after the bloody weddin' at least.

**Mark** (*rousing himself from his stupor and singing*)
                    The first mate's name was Carter
                    By God, he was a farter
                    When the wind wouldn't blow
                    And the ship wouldn't go
                    They'd send for Carter
                    The Starter to farter.

**Hamish** (*by reason of his conditioning, turning round and conducting*)
                    That was a very good song.
                    Sing us another one
                    Just like the other one
                    Sing us another one do.

**Peter** (*pointing at Hamish*) Bloody Hooray Henrys, who's he?
**Kevin** A mate of Mark's from the rugby club.
**Jimmy** I'm just going for a splash, man.

*Jimmy puts the joint down and exits*

*Nip looks to see no-one's looking then picks up the joint and starts smoking it furiously. Hamish brings the drinks over*

**Harry** No, Hitler warn't all wrong. I mean forget the Jews; that was bad but his other ideas—a car for every family, everyone in his place and burn the bloody Communists, that was right. Nothing wrong with that, the Tories believe in that as an Englishman's birthright.
**Mark** (*waking up*) Imobile, imobile, imo-imobile, imobile.
**Hamish** Imobile, imobile. (*He waves his hands about*)
**Nip** (*wheezing a bit*) By, them bloody fags are strong. I feel like I've put the wrong bloody head on. Whose round is it?
**Kevin** Mine, we'll 'ave one more 'ere, then we'll 'ave one at the *Catholic Club*, then go and find a night-club, come on sup up.
**Nip** Come on, let's have some service. Mine's a large rum with a splash of lemonade.

*The Lights fade to a Black-out*


### SCENE 5

"*The Catholic Club*"

*The Lights come up on Father Molloy sitting at a table. He is on the verge of total oblivion and is talking to a Man in more or less the same state*

**Father Molloy** An' didn't he say "Who wouldn't?" "Well," says I, "I don't care if it's illegal or not at all, ye can go pull the whole thing down, the whole shootin' match an' fergus to yer. Yez a gobeen."
**Man** There's a lot of them garages fall down on their own.
**Father Molloy** I'm not talking about garages at all. Your man was no where near awan, so maygo slaith.
**Man** What did he say?
**Father Molloy** Who?
**Man** Him.
**Father Molloy** What? Which him?
**Man** Your man who sold you the garage.
**Father Molloy** What d'ye mean?
**Man** The man wid de wooden leg that burnt down when the dog turned over the oil lamp.
**Father Molloy** What are ye talkin' about?
**Man** I don't know.
**Father Molloy** Then get another drink and shuttup talkin' like a broken radio.
**Man** Two large Bushmills.
**Father Molloy** Ye can understand that right enough.

*At this point, the crowd enter, minus Peter who has decided not to come.*
*They are now all fairly well oiled except Nip who still seems none the*
*worse for wear*

**Nip** Come on, whose round is it?
**Harry** 'S mine.
**Kevin** No, 's mine—you got the last one.
**Harry** I didn't, Amos gorrem.
**Hamish** Hamish—my name's Hamish.
**Kevin** 'Ello, Father.
**Father Molloy** Ah's th' very man in self . . . an' wall 'avin' boys—(*pause*)
   —'cos it's goods time s'any for a priscan buy sall drink. (*Translation:*
   *Ah it's the very man himself and what are you all having boys—'cos it's*
   *as good a time as any for a priest to buy you all a drink.*)
**Nip** (*the only one who has understood him*) Ah'll have a large rum an'
   lemonade.

*The Lights fade to a Black-out*


SCENE 6

*"The Can Can Club"*

*The Lights come up on the pavement area outside the club. A Bouncer is*
*standing there, punching his fists, looking massive and bored. Heavy rock*
*music is playing*

   *Nip saunters in, followed by Harry, Kevin and Mark, Father Molloy and*
   *Hamish, who are holding on to each other singing "Molly Malone"*

**Nip** Come on, get a move on. It'll be shut by the time we get there.
**Harry** They shouldn't have brought Father Molloy.
**Kevin** He'll be all right, they've covered his collar up. Anyway he doesn't
   know where he is.
**Bouncer** How many?
**Nip** Six, do you do reductions for party bookin's?
**Bouncer** (*looking suspiciously at Hamish, Mark and Father Molloy*) Are
   they all right?
**Kevin** They're just sleepy, they'll be all right.
**Bouncer** Well they'd better be or you're out the lot of ye.
**Nip** 'Ow much is the beer?
**Bouncer** Seventy-five p a pint.
**Nip** Bloody 'ell, I'm glad I'm not buyin'. Come on Amos, it's your round.

*They stagger past the Bouncer. The Lights cross-fade to the interior of the*
*Club. The music fades slightly*

   *The Bouncer exits*

*The others sit down, stumbling and burping and shouting*

**Nip** First thing first, where do we gerra drink?

**Kevin** Gerra waiter.

**Mark** "Wasona good ship Venus . . ." No, I know a good one . . . "She was poor but she was 'onest . . ."

**Harry** (*to a recumbent Hamish and Father Molloy*) And I said, "I don't care 'f y're a medical student, grab brushy brushy and mucho sweepy sweepy or it's sacky sacky, cardy, cardy, licky, licky P forty-five."

**Nip** (*standing up and looking round*) Ey, garçon—when you're ready.

*The Waiter enters*

**Waiter** Right, what is it?

**Nip** Large rum and lemonade and one, two, three, four, five whiskies and (*pointing at Harry*) he's paying. What time does it start then?

*The Waiter goes to the bar to get the drinks*

**Kevin** What?

**Nip** The show, you know, the strip.

**Kevin** Anytime now.

**Harry** (*to Kevin, indicating Hamish and Father Molloy*) These two buggers are spark out.

**Kevin** (*indicating Mark*) Superstud doesn't look much healthier.

*The Waiter comes over with a tray of drinks*

**Nip** Harry, cough up.

**Harry** How much?

**Waiter** Seven pounds thirty-five p.

**Harry** Jesus!

**Nip** Here watch your language, there's a priest here.

**Harry** (*to the Waiter*) Here, take it out of this. (*He hands him a ten-pound note*) And don't forget the change.

**Nip** Keep it, cock, it's his birthday. Do they have food here? I hate drinking on an empty stomach.

*The Waiter exits*

**Kevin** I don't know where you put it all—do you know how many you have had?

**Nip** No, but I'm not stopping now.

*The Bouncer enters*

**Bouncer** Right then, ladies and gentlemen, we're about to have our third girl of the evening.

**Nip** I haven't had me first yet.

**Bouncer** She's just come back from Moscow where she has been doing a successful tour of the Conservative clubs. Last week, she was the centre spread in the *Exchange and Mart*. May I present—the lovely Evette.

*Stripping music starts and Evette the Stripper comes on. She is clad in a bizarre feathery costume, a leather eye mask and carries a whip. She does a strip down to black leather thigh boots, a black leather G-string and bikini top. The effect should be comic rather than erotic*

*When she gets down to the briefest essentials, a blown-up rubber doll is thrown on stage. The Stripper begins fondling it, then whipping it. At this point Father Molloy wakes up*

**Father Molloy** (*screaming*) I'm dead, I'm dead and we're all in Hell, Holy Mother of God.

**Nip** Shurrup yer wozzack, yer'll gerrus throwed out.

**Kevin** Shurrim up, Dad.

**Father Molloy** All the fires and the torments! Beelzebub! I must've been knocked off me bike.

*The noise wakes up Mark and Hamish who stand up as the music stops abruptly*

*The Stripper walks off with her rubber doll*

*In the pause that ensues, Mark and Hamish go into "Swing Low Sweet Chariot", complete with rugby-club hand movements. The Bouncer comes over to them*

**Bouncer** Right, you lot—out. Let's 'ave you double-quick.

**Kevin** They'll be all right.

**Hamish** I'm going to be sick.

**Father Molloy** Oh God. Oh God, forgive me—in the hour of our death . . . (*He peters out*)

**Nip** Shut that bloody wart up.

**Bouncer** Out—(*grabbing Father Molloy*)—and you first, you mad swine.

**Father Molloy** I'm a priest, don't you know, a man of the cloth so to speak.

**Bouncer** An' I'm the Chief Rabbi—out, the lot of you before I start smashing some heads in.

*He throws them all out of the Club. Nip grabs the blow-up doll and chains from the wings as he goes*

*The Lights cross-fade to the pavement area. Hamish is bending over, throwing up, Mark is singing and Father Molloy's glasses are on the top of his head*

**Mark** (*singing*) The hairs on her dicky dido,
                 Hang down to her knees . . .

**Father Molloy** I can't see. I'm blin' . . . wheresmi glasses. (*He finds them and puts them on*)

**Nip** I were right enjoying that, she 'ad a right pair of Eartha Kitts, didn't she? At least ah finished me drink. (*He produces the doll and chains from behind his back*) 'Ere Kevin, look at this, ah pinched it on t'way out.

**Kevin** By 'eck we can have a laugh with this.

**Nip** Ay, we can that.

**Kevin** It's one of them that talks to you—look. (*He puts his fingers in the doll's mouth*)

**Nip** Don't put your fingers in there, it'll have yer bloody hand off, Eeh, there's some barmy buggers around isn't there?

**Mark** (*singing*) "I'm getting married in the morning . . ."

*Kevin looks at Nip. They both have the same thought*

**Kevin** Well, you can 'ave a practice run then.

*They chain Mark and the doll to the lamppost. Harry is standing to one side, obviously having a pee*

**Nip** Come on Amos, you can be the bridesmaid.

*They tie Hamish's jacket round his head. Hamish groans*

*Harry runs towards them, fastening his flies*

**Harry** There's some bobbies comin'.

**Nip** Bloody 'ell, we'd best undo 'im.

**Kevin** Where's the key then?

**Nip** I 'aven't gor it.

**Kevin** You pinched the bloody thing!

**Harry** (*seeing what has happened and panicking*) Well, I'd best be off home then.

*Harry rushes off*

**Nip** There's not much point in me stayin' either.

**Kevin** Me mam'll kill me.

*Nip and Kevin exit*

*At the same time, the Policeman and Policewoman enter*

*Father Molloy is praying on his knees, Hamish is throwing up and Mark has his arms round the doll*

**Policeman** Hello, lads. 'Aving a party, are we?

**Father Molloy** Godnsagers say me from all the hell anfires blumferlastinternities. (*Translation: God and his angels save me from all the hell-fire burning for lasting eternities.*)

*Hamish groans, looks up and groans again*

**Mark** (*singing*) "I'm getting married in the morning . . ."

*Mark inadvertently activates the doll which starts talking*

**Doll's Voice** Hello darling, fancy a good time? I'm all yours. Ooh, you are a big boy!

*Mark stares at the doll as—*

the Curtain *falls*

# ACT II

## SCENE 1

*The Ollerenshawes' living-room as before. Saturday morning*

*When the Lights come up, Nip is sitting on the settee drinking a mug of tea, with his shoes and jacket off, but wearing his flat cap*

*Peter comes in, wearing a shirt, socks and underpants. He turns the pictures to the wall, then crosses towards the kitchen*

**Peter** Hello, Grandad, what you doin' here so early?

*Peter goes off to the kitchen*

**Nip** I stayed on t'settee last night. We didn't gerrin till nearly three.
**Peter** (*off*) Did you have a good do?
**Nip** Ay, it would have been if Mark Greenhalgh hadn't pinched a rubber doll from *The Can Can Club* and our Kevin tied him to a lamppost.

*Peter enters L with a mug of tea*

**Peter** He didn't did he? Bloody stroll on!

*Kevin enters R, partly dressed, with his hand over his eyes, obviously suffering from kopfkrieg*

**Kevin** Oh God . . . oh God . . . my 'ead's like a pan of mince.
**Peter** Fancy a couple of runny eggs and some greasy bacon our Kevin?
**Kevin** (*sitting down*) Rotten sod. Ooh, what a night, I couldn't sleep. I had this terrible nightmare. I dreamt I chained Mark Greenhalgh to a lamppost with a blow-up rubber woman and the police arrested him.
**Peter** Grandad said you did.
**Nip** Ay, you did you dozy bugger.
**Kevin** You must be jokin'!
**Nip** It were round the corner from *The Can Can Club* you left him and Amos and Father Molloy.
**Kevin** (*jumping up*) Oh God. (*Then his head crashes in again*) Oh God. (*He sits down*)
**Peter** (*to Nip*) You never said anything about the fuzz.
**Nip** We never saw it; we got thrown out before she got 'er kecks off.
**Peter** I mean the police.
**Nip** The bobbies? Nay, we buggered off before they came.
**Peter** Well, that's the groom, best man and priest that've gone missing. Me mam'll go mad.
**Kevin** Oh, God she'll kill us.

**Peter** Hey, look, we'll have to do something or there'll be murder. Where were they staying last night?

**Kevin** *The Five-Barred Gate Motel* out on the by pass.

**Peter** I'll phone there and see if they're there. Do you know if they got arrested? (*He goes to the sideboard and looks up the telephone directory*)

**Kevin** No.

*Peter dials the number*

**Nip** I told you, we buggered off before they came.

**Kevin** Oh God, my head feels like a box of frogs.

**Peter** (*on the telephone*) Hello. Is that *The Five-Barred Gate*? . . . Hello, yes I can hear you, just about. What's that noise? . . . At this time in the morning? Could you tell me if Mr Mark Greenhalgh is staying there? . . . Mark Greenhalgh. . . . No, no, Mark . . . Mark, M . . . A . . . R . . . K. . . . Oh, oh yes, oh, I see. . . . Yes, well, yes yess, hmmm, oh, well can you put me through to his room? (*To Kevin and Nip*) The police brought them back an hour ago. There's some Tibetan Monks staying there for a ping-pong convention and they're all praying in the lobby or something. I can hardly hear. (*On the telephone*) Hello. Hello, is that Mark Greenhalgh? It's Peter Ollerenshawe here. . . . Deirdre's brother. . . . Yes Deirdre. Are you OK? . . . Oh, oh Jesus. . . . Oh. . . . (*Stifling laughter*) Yes, yes. OK, we'll be out there for half-eleven. Cars at twelve, OK? . . . Yes. OK. . . . No, we're getting changed here. . . . OK, yes, you'd better had, OK . . . Cheers. See you then. (*He puts the telephone down and almost explodes with laughter*) Oh, my God. I'd love to have been there. It must have been like the three stooges.

**Nip** What happened?

**Kevin** Don't tell me. I don't want to know.

**Peter** The police found Mark chained to a blow-up rubber doll in Market Place, like you said. But when they tried to take him in, Hamish hit one of the bobbies.

**Nip** Amos? Good owd Amos. He's not as wet as ah thowt he was.

**Peter** It was a policewoman he hit. They were doing him for assault but they let him off because of Mark's dad being who he is.

**Kevin** Oh my God, me mam'll go mad.

**Peter** Anyway the fuzz rang for reinforcements after Hamish got nasty and when the meat-wagon arrived, Father Molloy who for some reason or another kept thinkin' he was in Hell, threw himself into the ornamental pond outside the library saying they were devils and were after him. He pulled the head off one of the angels on the fountain and threw it through the window of the Tourist Information Centre.

**Nip** Bloody 'ell.

**Peter** They were doing him for being drunk and disorderly but they let him off too.

**Kevin** 'Ave they let them all out?

**Peter** Yes. They couldn't charge Mark with anything except drunk and disorderly and they dropped that because of his dad.

**Nip** What about the doll?

**Peter** Well, *The Can Can Club* denied they'd ever seen it, said they ran a respectable art revue. So as far as the police are concerned, it's Mark's own property.

**Kevin** Thank God for that.

**Peter** And they said the whole affair won't go any further so his mam and dad won't hear about it. Youthful high spirits, they called it. Youthful high spirits, he's twenty-bloody-six.

**Kevin** Where's me dad?

**Nip** Gone for the flowers on his bike.

**Kevin** I was supposed to go.

**Nip** You weren't up. So he went to get out of the way. The women have gone to the hairdressers.

**Peter** Bloody typical intit!

**Kevin** What is?

**Peter** A story drops right into me lap containing sex, religion, crime and corruption in high places and I can't use it because me own family's involved in it up to the armpits.

**Kevin** What d'you mean?

**Peter** Two Hooray Henrys and a drunken priest are found falling about with a bondage sex doll. One of the Hooray Henrys hits an officer of the law and the priest destroys corporation property and all charges are dropped because the Chief Inspector is in the same Masonic Lodge as the number one Hooray Henry's father and I can't use the story because my stupid sister is marrying same number one Hooray Henry and involved in the whole plot is my drunkard brother, my Fascist father and my geriatric delinquent grandfather.

**Nip** Less of the geriatric, there's nothing wrong with my bowels.

**Peter** That's incontinent.

**Nip** It's got bugger all to do with t'Common Market.

**Kevin** Well thank God they got away anyway.

*There is the sound of dustbins being knocked over, off, followed by something being dropped, a shot, then a dog howling*

> *Harry enters* R, *again in full motor-bike kit and carrying boxes of flowers and a gun*

**Harry** Well, it won't crap on our path again.

**Nip** 'Ave yer killed it?

**Harry** No, but it won't sit down for a good bit. It won't stop running till Bolton. It's got half a pound of lead under its tail.

**Kevin** Did you hear what 'appened to Mark then?

**Harry** Yes, I called at *The Five-Barred Gate* on the way back to give 'em their buttonholes. The'ad a lucky do, didn't they?

**Nip** Well, it were only a bachelor-night do. You expect a bit of nonsense on a bachelor do.

**Harry** Hamish has got seventeen stitches for his bit of nonsense.

**Kevin** Yer what?

**Harry** He took a swing at a policewoman and she laid him out with a judo throw. He cut his head on the minute-hand of the floral clock in the town gardens. (*He indicates with his hands*) Another ten minutes he'd have cut his throat open. That bloody hotel was full of Chinks wailing and falling about on little mats. Bloody barmy. What're they all doin' over here? Hitler wouldn't 'ave 'ad it, they'd 'ave kept their fallin' about and loud bangin' for their own country and not done it over here.

*Deirdre and Edith enter* R, *carrying shopping bags. They are followed by Kirstene and Wendy, the bridesmaids. They have all just had their hair done. They are all very shaken*

**Edith** Oh, my God. I feel terrible. (*She collapses on to the settee*)

**Deirdre** (*sitting down*) I think I'm going to be sick.

**Edith** I've never seen anything like it. I hope it's not an omen. My mother always believed in omens.

**Deirdre** Oh Mother, do you think it is?

**Peter** What's happened?

**Edith** We were just coming back from the 'airdressers in a taxi . . .

**Kirstene** Ay, we were, Uncle.

**Wendy** And do you know what happened?

**Peter** What the bloody hell happened?

**Deirdre** And next door's dog shot across the road in front of a bus.

**Harry** Sweet Jesus Christ. (*He crosses himself*)

**Edith** The bus swerved and went straight through the baker's window. (*To the bridesmaids*) Nip upstairs and get changed, loves.

**Kirstene** Hurry up Wendy, I'm dying to go to t'lavvy.

*Wendy and Kirstene exit* R

**Harry** Was anybody hurt?

**Deirdre** They thought the driver's throat was cut because he was such a mess but it was only jam out of the strawberry flans. The dog's dead but nobody else is hurt.

**Harry** Did the bus hit it?

**Edith** No, it were running round in circles trying to bite its own tail and it just ran into a wall and fell over and dropped dead in a tray of eclairs. Eh, I could murder a cup of tea. Me nerves are all shot and I've got one of me 'eads comin' on.

**Harry** Our Peter, make your mam a cup of tea while we get changed will you.

**Peter** Ay, all right.

*Peter exits* L *to the kitchen*

*Harry, Nip and Kevin exit* R, *Harry hiding his gun behind his back*

**Deirdre** I feel really faint.

**Edith** It's the last time I go in that baker's. I don't think I could face another eclair as long as I live. Here, we'll have a drop of brandy, that'll sort us out. (*She gets up and pours out two large brandies*) Chuck me one of your dad's fags, love.

*Deirdre takes a cigarette from the packet on the mantelpiece and passes it to Edith. Edith thinks for a minute*

Eh love, when ah think it doesn't seem ten minutes since I was rockin'
you on me knee and now you're off gettin' married and ah don't suppose
it'll be long before you'll be rockin' your own babies on your knee.

**Deirdre** Not me, Mother.

**Edith** Yer what? You're not thinkin' of using anythin' are you? We may
not 'ave fish on Fridays, but it doesn't mean we've got to 'ave rubber
on Saturdays.

**Deirdre** Oh, Mother.

**Edith** And they say one in three of them's got a hole in it anyway just to
keep the population up. You just want to be careful what you're doing
girl. None of that gerrin' off at Bury instead of stoppin' on till Bolton.
That's how you got here.

**Deirdre** Mother, sometimes I wonder where you get it from.

**Edith** (*in a rascally mood now*) You want to try the biscuit-tin method.

**Deirdre** What's the biscuit-tin method?

**Edith** You do it standin' up with him stood on a biscuit tin then when
his face goes red, and his ears wobble and his eyes cross, you kick it
away from under him.

*They laugh then Edith recollects what she's just said*

Oooh, wor am ah saying in front of Sacred 'Art. (*She looks*) Mother of
God, it's turned round—it's a sign.

**Deirdre** So's the Queen. She can't be upset as well. It's our Peter, he's
always turning them round.

*Peter comes in L with a mug of tea*

**Edith** I'll kill you one of these days. (*She cracks him one*) Get upstairs and
get changed it's nearly half-past ten, and you have to be at the church
by quarter-past twelve.

**Peter** OK. I'll hurry the others up as well.

*Peter exits R*

**Edith** (*turning the pictures round*) Bloody kids, they drive me mad. Are you
not planning to start a family right away then?

**Deirdre** Well, Mark and I thought later on, when he's taken over his
father's business, he might want a son to hand it on to.

**Edith** Is Ron Greenhalgh retiring then?

**Deirdre** Well, not right away of course, but I don't think it'll be long.
They've got a lovely bungalow at Abersoch and Mrs Greenhalgh sort of
hinted that it would be nice when they would be able to spend more time
there.

**Edith** Eh, I am glad for you. You seem to have everything you want. A
nice, handsome husband (or he will be anyway), a good job, a lovely
bungalow up Moorside and a honeymoon in Bermuda.

**Deirdre** Wait till I show you what I've got to wear on my wedding night.
(*She opens her shopping bag and takes out a sexy black négligé*)

**Edith** (*taking it and holding it up*) You want to put some fur on the bottom
to keep your neck warm.

**Deirdre** (*putting it back in her bag*) Mother, you are common.

**Edith** (*pulling out a pair of scanty briefs*) And look at these. There isn't enough here to cover me birthmark let alone keep me air of mystery intact. You'll catch your death of cold in these.

**Deirdre** Mother, put them away.

**Edith** I hope he hasn't got sharp nails—he'll ladder them. Just look at them. Well, he won't need much imagination anyway. My mother always used to say, "Keep the bone and the dog'll follow." Things have changed since then.

**Deirdre** Oooh, don't mention dogs. (*She snatches the panties back and tries to stuff them away*)

**Edith** Ooh my God, look at the time. (*Shouting off* R) Come on, you lot, let's be having you.

*Peter, Harry, Nip and Kevin enter* R, *dressed in grey morning suits and top hats. They all look fairly reasonable except Peter, whose long hair sticks out, and Nip, whose suit doesn't fit properly. He still has his flat 'at on and carries his topper in his hand*

Well, you look proper gentlemen.

**Peter** I've never felt so daft in my life. I hate suits—real bloody bourgeois, they rub between my legs, I'm goin' to put some talc down the pants.

*Peter exits* R

**Nip** Did you get me bloody measurements right? There's more ballroom here than in Blackpool Tower.

**Edith** Course I did, they were on that bit of paper you gave me!

**Nip** I never gave you a bit of paper. You wrote it down.

**Edith** Well . . . I've got it here in me purse. (*She produces a piece of paper from her purse*) Look.

**Nip** (*taking it*) Let's see. That's not me measurements, that's for some lino for round the pedestal in me bathroom.

**Edith** Well, you don't look too bad. (*To Deirdre*) Have you any pins we can sort him out with?

**Deirdre** I'll get some.

*Deirdre exits* R

*The next part of the action should have as much confusion as possible, as they all rush around trying to get ready, coming in and going out quickly*

**Kevin** Have you got your garter?

**Nip** Who me? You can't hold me pants up with garters.

**Kevin** Not you, our Deirdre.

*Deirdre enters* R

**Deirdre** Yes, it's in the drawer, I can't find any.

**Edith** Come on, 'urry up, get your carnations on. I'll go and look.

*Edith exits*

*Kevin, Nip and Harry put on their buttonholes*

**Deirdre** Where's them new tights I just bought? (*She takes a packet of tights from her bag*)

*Deirdre exits* R

**Harry** Did you check with the photographer?

*Edith enters* R

**Edith** The cake's gone, 'asn't it?
**Harry** Who took it?
**Edith** I thought you picked it up.
**Harry** 'Ow could I on me bike?

*Harry exits* R

*Deirdre enters* R

**Deirdre** Oh, Mother, everything's going wrong.
**Edith** Don't panic, don't panic. Oh me head. Where's me tablets?

*Edith and Deirdre exit* R

**Nip** (*holding his trousers up*) Bugger the bloody cake, will someone pin me trousers up?

*Peter enters* R, *rubbing his crotch and carrying a tin of scouring powder*

**Peter** Who left that scouring powder in me bedroom? I've put half a hundredweight of it down me trouser legs.

*Peter exits* ⎱

*Harry enters* R

**Harry** Has anybody seen my Oxo tin that I keep me maggots in?
**Kevin** What the bloody hell do you want maggots for now?
**Harry** I've left me spare bike keys in the maggot tin and I can't find me others.
**Kevin** You're not going on the bike like that.
**Harry** I'm going for the cake.

*Harry exits* L

*Edith enters* R *and sticks a pin in Nip*

**Nip** Ay, go easy lass, you nearly pinned me liver to me weddin' tackle then.
**Edith** Well, stop jumpin' about then. (*She pins his trousers up*)

*Deirdre enters* R

**Deirdre** (*as she enters*) My new underskirt's in a bag somewhere. (*She picks up her shopping bag*)

*Deidre exits* R

*Harry enters* L

**Harry** I still can't find the Oxo tin. She's probably thrown it away. She throws everything away she does.

*Peter enters* R

**Kevin** Look, we'll pick up the bloody cake on the way to pick up Mark. Drop it off at the Masonic Hall and go on to *The Five-Barred Gate*.

**Harry** On my motor bike?

**Kevin** No, in the taxi.

**Peter** (*putting on his carnation*) Did you order the taxi?

**Kevin** I thought you were doing that.

**Nip** (*putting his hat on top of his cap*) I feel flamin' daft with this hat on.

**Edith** Well take your cap off first.

**Peter** The car's here.

**Harry** What for?

**Edith** To take you lot to *The Five-Barred Gate*, you dumbos. I ordered it this morning.

*Deirdre enters* R, *wearing a dressing-gown*

**Deirdre** Mother, can you give me a hand?

**Nip** (*picking up the scanty briefs*) What's these?

**Deirdre** Grandad, they're mine.

**Nip** Bloody 'ell. We used to have more than that for keepin' flies from gerrin' in the milk jug.

**Edith** Out, the lot of you.

**Nip** I'm ready. (*He takes a bottle of brandy from the bar and puts it under his jacket*)

**Edith** And don't forget the buttonholes for the groom and the best man.

**Harry** They've already got 'em.

*Harry, Kevin, Peter and Nip exit* R, *shouting "See you in church" as they go*

*Kirstene and Wendy enter* R, *wearing their bridesmaids' dresses*

**Edith** 'Ey by, but you do look bonny the pair of you don't they, Deirdre?

**Deirdre** Ay. (*Then realizing*) Mother, where's me dad gone?

**Edith** The daft bugger. Must'ave forgot he's givin' you away.

*Edith runs out* R

(*Off*) Harry, Harry, come back you soft devil.

**Deirdre** Come on, girls, give me a hand, I'll have to hurry—it's nearly half-past.

*Deirdre and the girls pick up their dresses and exit* R

*The Lights fade to a Black-out*

SCENE 2

*The Church*

*There are pews at either side and an altar in the middle. Perhaps a couple of*

*stained glass windows could be flown in to suggest a church. Bells peal and
organ music plays*

*Mark and Hamish enter, walk down the aisle and take their places in
front of the altar. Hamish has a plaster on his head*

*The families and guests gradually enter and fill the pews, the Ollerenshawes
on the left and the Greenhalghs on the right. They nod and wave to each
other*

*Muriel Greenhalgh blows a kiss to Mark and dabs her eyes. The Light fades
to a spot on Muriel and the organ music fades*

**Muriel** Muriel Greenhalgh. Mother of the handsome groom, and as you
can see, I have been a bit of a looker myself, in my time. Chairwoman
of the Townswomen's Guild and on the board of several local charities.
Because of my position in the community, I am into do-gooding in a big
way. There is just one thing I don't like to be reminded of and that is that
I was born and brought up in Jubilee Terrace, the next street to the
Ollerenshawes—well, people might think that I am not used to the best,
and I am. Rover cars, Jaeger clothes, Capo di Monte, Waterford
Crystal, Poggenpöhl kitchens and holidays abroad. Dress: Rotary Club
chic, mink stoles for Masonic evenings, underwear from Marks and
Spencer, very like the Queen really. Pet Hate: Common people. Hobbies:
My social life, and gratifyingly finding that I'm still attractive to the
opposite sex. Religion: Margaret Thatcher. Guilty Secrets: Forty-seven
American airmen, seven refuse-disposal operatives, six Cosmos tour
couriers and one door-to-door brush salesman. But who's counting?

*The Lights come up on the church. Organ music begins and plays throughout
the following section, swelling and then dying*

Don't look now, Ronald, but they all look drunk. And that woman in
the third pew, isn't that their cousin from Barnsley who ran off with
another woman. They do seem a coarse bunch.
**Ronald** Our Mark's not marrying the family, he's marrying the girl and
she's all right.
**Muriel** Well, I'm not going to go through it all again, but he could have
chosen somebody better.
**Ronald** Now Muriel, this isn't the time or the place.
**Muriel** But he could have found somebody from somewhere better than
Bessemer Estate.
**Ronald** When they've married they won't live on Bessemer Estate and if
I'm any judge of human nature, that young girl won't want anything
more to do with her family than she has to once she's married. She
wants to climb up in the world and she'll get behind Mark and push.
**Muriel** I'd still rather he'd married that Elswick girl from the water-ski
club.
**Ronald** Here's her mother now.

*Edith enters on Kevin's arm*

*Muriel and Ronald nod and smile to them. Edith and Kevin take their places*

**Edith** (*to Kevin*) Stuck-up cow.
**Muriel** (*to Ronald*) That hat looks ridiculous.
**Edith** (*to Kevin*) That hat looks bloody ludicrous on her.
**Muriel** Those shoes don't match that suit at all.
**Edith** Those shoes clash with that blouse.
**Muriel** I do wish our Mark had done better for himself.
**Edith** I think our Deirdre could have done a lot better for herself.
**Muriel** (*smiling at Edith then talking to Ronald*) Common as muck.
**Edith** (*smiling back at her and then to Kevin*) All fur coat and no knickers.
   She only came from Cloughbottoms, Jubilee Street—same as the rest
   of us.

*Father Molloy enters, looking very much the worse for wear. He has a
black eye and his glasses are held together with sticking plaster and
Sellotape*

*The organ strikes up "Here Comes the Bride"*

**Nip** (*turning round*) Here they are.

*All the guests turn their heads*

   *Deirdre enters on Harry's arm, and they walk down the aisle, followed by
   the bridesmaids*

*The wedding takes place in a series of flashes—the action freezes periodically
as the characters think out loud. (It could also be done as in the Oldham production, with a series of back-projected slides of the wedding photographs of
the event.) As Deirdre and Harry reach the altar, "Here Comes the Bride"
fades into hymn music, which continues faintly in the background throughout the ceremony. The action freezes*

**Edith** (*thinking out loud*) She does look lovely.
**Muriel** I think I'd have at least got real lace. It looks cheap and nasty that
   dress.

*The action continues. When Father Molloy speaks, it should be made very
echoey, if possible, so that it is almost impossible to hear what he's saying*

**Father Molloy** Dearly beloved brethern. Weregard hereday to wiznets the
   joining 'n' marge of these two young peeble. (*He looks up from the altar*)

*The action freezes*

**Ronald** He sounds drunk.
**Kevin** He sounds pissed already.
**Father Molloy** Holy Mother o'God, I think I'm still full of the drink.

*The action continues, with Father Molloy speaking the wedding ceremony,
barely audible under the organ music. Hamish takes out the ring. The action
freezes*

**Muriel** Hamish has got a plaster on his head!

**Hamish** Oh Lord, my head's throbbing.

*The action continues. At the appropriate moment, Mark and Deirdre kiss, and then pull back a bit. The action freezes again*

**Edith** At least she's marrying someone with a bit of money if nothing else.
**Muriel** She's got him now just where she wants him.
**Hamish** Well, that's him tied down with his little wifey. No more rugger-club binges for matey.
**Kevin** I wonder what he sees in our Deirdre?
**Mark** She looks like a . . . like a . . . like an angel.
**Deirdre** Isn't he handsome—and won't we make a lovely couple. I'm so happy.
**Peter** Just like something out of bloody *Woman's Own*. All knitting patterns, weddin's, the Royal Family and adverts for ointment for personal membrane itching.
**Harry** I think I left the lights on on me bike.
**Nip** I wish they'd hurry up. I'm dying for a drink. I've got a mouth like the inside of a navvy's welly.

*The action continues*

**Father Molloy** We will now go into the sacrilige and sign the regicide.

*Mark, Deirdre, Hamish and Wendy exit with Father Molloy to sign the register*

*The action freezes*

**Kevin** He's signing his bloody life away like Kevin Keegan.
**Harry** I wonder how much these registrars get paid? It must be a cushy job, you only work Saturdays.
**Ronald** They've got it sewn up these Roman Catholics. Birth control, idolatry, the lot. Look at these statues, just like a lot of pagans.
**Muriel** Well he's done it now. He's made his bed and he'll have to lie on it. She may be all right in the long run, but I doubt it. She smelt money that girl.
**Ronald** Still, it'll be nice to have grandchildren to hand the business on to.
**Muriel** If she thinks she's pushing me off to that bungalow in Abersoch she's got another think coming. It's damp and besides I hate the Welsh, they always talk Welsh when they find out you're English in the shops.
**Nip** Are they signing the Magna Charta in there or what?

*The action continues. The organ strikes up "The Wedding March"*

*Deirdre, Mark, Hamish and Wendy enter with Father Molloy*

*Peter and Kevin go to the back as ushers and the wedding procession comes down the aisle and exits*

*As the guests start to leave, the Lights fade to a Black-out*

SCENE 3

*The Reception at the Masonic Hall*

*The Lights come up on the reception area, where tables and chairs are set out.
Deirdre and Mark are waiting to receive their guests*

*The guests, apart from Muriel and Harry, enter and are received by the
bride and groom in the following order*

**Hamish** Well, one thing I'm going to do first and that's kiss the blushing
bride. (*He kisses Deirdre*)

**Deirdre** Oh Hamish, what have you done to your head?

**Hamish** Cut myself shaving, little lady, not to worry. Worse things happen
at sea.

**Edith** Oh Deirdre, you do look nice. It did go well. It was a lovely service.
(*Looking at Mark*) Oooh, let me look at him—I wish I was twenty years
younger.

**Mark** Ha, ha. (*Uneasily*) You're only saying that, Edith.

**Edith** Ay yer right, anyway I'll go an' 'ave a drink. I think I've got one of
me 'eads comin' on . . . ooh! (*She goes to the table and takes a sherry*)

**Ronald** It went wonderfully and I'm very pleased for you both. Good luck,
son and don't let it be too long before we've another generation of
Greenhalghs to carry on.

**Nip** Well, let them get their clothes off first.

*Ronald kisses Deirdre*

Here let me kiss the bride and get a drink. You're 'oldin' t'bloody queue
up. All the best, love. (*He kisses Deirdre*)

**Deirdre** Thanks, Grandad.

**Nip** (*to Mark*) And ah must say you did better than you did at rehearsals
last night. (*He goes to get a drink from the table*)

**Deirdre** What rehearsals?

**Mark** I think your Grandad's a bit mixed up.

*Muriel enters with Harry in a flounce of self-righteousness*

**Muriel** You know I think that driver was trying to crush my hat the way
he flung us round those corners. Oh, there they are. Mark love—and
Deirdre. It went wonderfully and such a quaint service. I suppose all you
Catholics have your services in Latin.

**Deirdre** It was in English. Well, Irish sort of English.

**Muriel** Really. I must need my ears syringeing. Oh, your dress is lovely!
Where did you get it from?

**Deirdre** Mrs Williams made it in the High Street. She makes all the best
wedding dresses. You often see her stuff in *North Country Life*.

**Muriel** Really! I must look out for her more often. I might get her to
make something for myself. We've got a Townswomen's Guild dinner-

dance this month and Ronald has a big dealers' dinner in Morecambe
as well as his Grand Master's Year coming up——

*As Muriel gabbles on, Harry is standing looking lost and in need of a drink*

**Harry** (*kissing Deirdre*) All the best, love.

**Muriel** —so I'll need some new outfits. Have you got all your stuff packed
for Bermuda? I so love Bermuda. The sunset over Spanish Point is just
like a picture . . .

**Nip** (*blustering in with a glass of sherry*) 'Ere missus, gerra drink and get
some grub, Me belly thinks me throat's cut.

**Deirdre** I rather don't think you've met my grandfather, Mrs Greenhalgh.

**Nip** She 'as but she weren't Mrs Greenhalgh then, she war Muriel Lees
and she worked in Jackson's sellin' ends of rolls and fire salvage.

**Muriel** (*losing ground*) Oh isn't it funny you should remember that, I'd
almost forgotten those days, doesn't time fly . . .

**Nip** Ay, there were a lot of flyers round in them days—Yanks mainly.

**Muriel** (*sensing danger*) Well, I think Mr Ollerenshawe and I will get some
food and not hold everybody up any longer.

*They all turn towards the table*

**Nip** Come on Amos, get things goin'. It's your job as best man.

*Hamish ushers the guests to their seats at the tables, seating them as is
usual at wedding dinners. (It could also be done as a buffet, with the actors
moving about.) Nip sits next to Muriel Greenhalgh*

*Father Molloy enters*

**Father Molloy** God bless all here. (*He sits next to Nip*)

**Peter** Are you all right, Father?

**Father Molloy** Yes, thank you. (*He wobbles downstage, taking a bottle and
a glass with him*)

*The Lights fade to a spot on Father Molloy, as he gives a totally incompre-
hensible monologue*

Far Finbar Aidan Molloy. Kilshermock County Mayo. Educated
Maynooth and come tinglan asprees Holy Roman Church. (*After a long
pause*) An' sany mangan see likes a drop of the crathur an' why no? A
man has a drop or two time an' why no? (*He waves the bottle about*)
Church roof an' new vestments—big worry, marry all people baptoise
lill chillen. (*He pauses and wobbles about*) Alla gan say's—(*he pauses*)
—Slainthe. (*He raises his glass and wobbles back to his seat*)

*The Lights come up on the reception*

**Edith** Will you say Grace for us, Father?

**Father Molloy** An', of course, at a time like that not better than a professional for handling the business in hand fyetake me meanin'—(*he
puts his hands together*)—an' anyone wishin' to partake of it for the
betterment of the occasion that's in it why a glass or two is a fine thing.

**Harry** Amen.

**Father Molloy** I haven't said it yet. Are ye drunk or daft or both? Blessens old ord where my grifts whichrbout receive from thy bounty through Christ our Lordamen. (*Translation: Bless us, O Lord, and these thy gifts which we are about to receive from thy bounty, through Christ our Lord, Amen.*)

*They all say "Amen" and begin to clatter the plates about. A lot of wine flows into Father Molloy's and Nip's glasses. The conversations which follow should flash about disjointedly as most dinner-table conversations do*

**Muriel** I'm so glad they were free to have us here at the Masonic Hall, it's such a cosy room.

**Edith** Well, we could'ave gone—(*here she puts on a few airs*)—to *The Old Mill Lodge* or the Conservative Club, but I thought we might be a little more homely here. The décor is rather nice, do you not think?

**Nip** I wouldn't have gone in t' Con Club any road.

**Kevin** Why not, they sell ale don't they?

**Nip** That were the 'eadquarters of the strike breakers in nineteen twenty-six. Students used to sign on there to drive trams: till me and Eddy Charlesworth dug up the drains and put dead rats in the ventilators.

**Edith** That's enough, Father.

**Ronald** Don't you like the Conservatives then?

**Nip** I met a generous Tory once.

**Ronald** (*forcing a smile*) Oh ay?

**Nip** He had diarrhoea.

*This is greeted by a mixture of laughs and cold reception, followed by a brief silence that Father Molloy breaks with a totally incomprehensible statement*

**Father Molloy** An' when ye think about it why shouldn't a man wear anythin' at all to do with wan thing nor the other neither religion or the politics if in God's eyes under the skin?

*There is a pregnant silence for a few seconds*

**Muriel** Hear, hear, people have to learn that they'll only get what they work for in this world. There's far too many people expect feather bedding. Things don't fall out of the sky.

**Nip** American airmen do.

**Deirdre** Is your soup nice, Grandad?

**Nip** Not bad, it doesn't taste much. I reckon t'chicken must have farted in it. (*He knocks his roll off the table*) Bugger it, I've dropped me roll. (*He climbs down under the table*)

*Father Molloy, thinking he's going for a secret drink, goes down after him, taking a bottle of brandy with him*

**Father Molloy** I'll bring a bottle . . .

*The conversation continues on over them and they are hidden from view for a while by the table-cloth*

**Muriel** Tell me, Mr Ollerenshawe, are you busy at Pussyfoot?

**Harry** Well, we'll be a bit slack till Christmas, and then the rush'll start.
**Edith** I know someone who works at your garage, Mrs Greenhalgh.
**Muriel** That's nice.
**Harry** Who's that then?
**Edith** Well, you know that girl that our Doreen's Ellen were at school
with who ran off with the PE teacher, Mr Clarkson. Him who took all
the girls on the outward bound courses. Well, his sister's cousin used to
have the corner shop at the bottom of Edge Lane, you know, the one
opposite that cobbler's where the bloke got sent to prison for stealing
underwear off washing lines and well, their Derek's wife gorra part time
job at Greenhalgh Motors when the children went to school. Oh, she
knows your Mark as well, 'cos I saw her in t'butchers last Wednesday,
or was it Thursday.
**Muriel** Oh! Oh! (*Shrieking*) Something's got my leg. Oh my God.

*Nip and Father Molloy emerge from under the table*

**Nip** We were looking for me bread roll and he thowt it were your ankle.
**Ronald** Is he schizophrenic?
**Nip** No he's Roman Catholic. He's all right. He's just tired. He's been
doin' a lot of baptisms and some of them babies are heavy.
**Harry** (*changing the subject*) Well you seem to be doing well at Greenhalgh
Motors, Ronald.
**Ronald** Yes, I can't complain, Harold. It seems a long time since we got
back in nineteen forty-five with our demob suits and our gratuities. (*He
moves downstage to do his bit*)

*The Lights fade to a spot on Ronald*

Ronald Greenhalgh. Storekeeper, Preston Barracks nineteen thirty-nine
to nineteen forty-five, made nearly one thousand pounds selling army
blankets and webbing back to the suppliers and working the black
market in the North. I'm a self-made man and proud of it. Business is
business. It's a cruel world. Religion: The Masons, the golf club and
money! I started off with one car on a bomb site, now I have a business
worth a million. Used to like the ladies but more concerned with the
sensuality of the bank vaults now. Guilty Secrets: None—but I don't
sleep too well at nights.

*The Lights come up on the reception at Ronald returns to his seat*

(*Going back into action*) Yes, Harold, I can't complain. They say there's
not much money about, but people still go for class cars. I've got a
waiting list twelve months long for my top models.
**Harry** British cars 'ave 'ad it, the unions 'ave ruined 'em. You used to be
able to buy a car and it'd last you ten, fifteen, twenty years. Now you're
lucky if they last two. Hitler 'ad the right idea with that Volkswagen. One
for every family. Hitler wouldn't 'ave 'ad unions.

*As Muriel speaks, Kevin looks at Peter, shaking his head*

**Muriel** You're right, Mr Ollerenshawe. The trouble with some people is that they think that the world owes them a living. All these scroungers on the dole.

**Peter** (*fairly well drunk now*) I see they just spent a quarter of a million redecoratin' Princess Anne's stables.

**Muriel** Well, don't you think it's worth it to have a Royal Family?

**Edith** I think the Queen does a wonderful job. Where would we be without 'er.

**Peter** Why?

**Muriel** Something to look up to surely.

**Edith** She's a figure-head. She stands for everything Britain stands for.

**Peter** Ay. Arab sheiks, Wimpy bars, cruise missiles, Japanese cars, American money, General Motors, space invaders, fall-out shelters and the rich gettin' richer and the poor gerrin' poorer.

**Ronald** You're just cynical young man, it's just youth, Mrs Ollerenshawe. Fine ideals are all right, but in the end it all comes down to Human Nature, dog eat dog.

**Hamish** (*to Peter*) If you think like that why don't you go and live in Russia with all the other Commies?

**Peter** Because I like it here. I just want to make it a fairer place to live in that's all, pal.

**Mark** You'll never do it. People are basically stupid. They need leading.

**Peter** Do you realize three per cent of the population still owns ninety per cent of the wealth of this country?

**Edith** What's that got to do with the Queen?

**Peter** She's one of the bloody three per cent.

**Deirdre** He just wants to start an argument.

**Ronald** (*patronizingly*) No, we're just having a discussion, that's all.

**Nip** (*breaking in*) I met Prince Philip once.

**Mark** Where was that?

**Nip** I were workin' at Grimey Pit and he came to open a new shower and washing screens. He came over to talk to me.

**Deirdre** What did he say to you?

**Nip** He asked me how I liked the new showers.

**Kevin** What did you say?

**Nip** I said "Lovely thanks but I still can't get the coal dust out of me balls!"

**Edith** Father! Eee, ah'm sorry, Mrs Greenhalgh.

**Muriel** It's all right, Mrs Ollerenshawe. I expect it's his age.

**Deirdre** Shouldn't someone read the telegrams.

**Hamish** Oh gosh yes. I nearly forgot, I was so caught up in the—erm interesting conversation.

**Kevin** ⎫
**Peter** ⎬ (*together; mocking him*) Oh gosh yes!

*Hamish gabbles through a number of telegrams, continually heckled by Kevin and Peter*

**Hamish** "Wishing you all the best—Uncle Tom and Aunty Freda."

**Edith** Oooh, that's nice of your Uncle Tom isn't it?

**Kevin**⎱(*together*) Very nice, yes, lovely, very nice.
**Peter**⎰

**Hamish** "May all your troubles be little ones—Maurice and Sybil."

**Muriel** Lovely.

**Kevin**⎱(*together*) Maurice and Sybil, how super. Absolutely topping.
**Peter**⎰

**Hamish** "Put your things together and have a good time—the Lads at the Rugger Club."

**Kevin**⎱ (*together*) ⎰Oh, the Lads at the Rugger Club. Rah rah oggie oggie
**Peter**⎰            ⎱bloody oggie.

*Edith has had enough of it and blows her top*

**Edith** Right, shut up the pair of you! I'll bloody well kill you when I get you home!

*There is a pregnant silence from everyone*

I'm sorry.

**Hamish** Right, well, it seems that today I have two jobs to do. First I have to thank Mark on behalf of the bridesmaids for a speech he hasn't made yet.

*Laughter*

But before that I have to propose a toast to the bride and groom. I've known Mark for a long time now. Ever since we started at prep school together, and he's always been a sterling chap.

*"Hear, hears" from Harry, who suddenly realizes he's the only one and stops*

One of those chaps one can rely on in any emergency.

**Harry** (*loudly*) Hear, hear. (*He smiles round the table*)

**Hamish** But more than anything he's been a team man. I know that this is a league town, but you'll have to forgive us union men if we mix a few metaphors (*he smiles condescendingly around*) when I say that together with Deirdre, Mark has started a new team up and that from now on they'll be a team together, the Mark and Deirdre team.

*"Hear, hears" and banging on the table from Harry, Ronald, Edith, Kevin and Peter. Muriel smiles. Mark and Deirdre exchange loving smiles. Nip and Father Molloy steal drinks*

Now they may find that life's a game that the referee's back's turned some time and there's a bit of needling going on in the scrum——

**Nip** (*to Father Molloy*) What the bloody 'ell's 'e on about?

**Father Molloy** Asm glow.

**Hamish** (*continuing uninterrupted*)—but so long as the passes from the line-out are straight and true and so long as they're shoulder to shoulder, I know that when the game is coming thick and fast, they'll ruck together.

**Nip** (*in a loud whisper*) What did he say then? Did 'ee say "fuck", I could swear 'ee said "fuck".

**Edith** Father, shurrup.

**Nip** I've never 'eard a weddin' speech like that, 'ee's puddled that Amos. 'Ee's as much sense as a toad 'as feathers.
**Edith** Father, shurrup.
**Nip** He said "fuck", not me.
**Hamish** It only remains for me to propose a toast to today's lovely couple. Ladies and gentlemen. I give you Deirdre and Mark.

*All rise and toast Deirdre and Mark. When they sit down again, Muriel squeals and jumps up*

**Nip** (*by way of explanation*) She sat on me 'and.

*Mark stands to make his speech, pulling out a piece of paper from his pocket*

**Nip** (*still explaining to Muriel*) I had me 'and on t'chair an' you sat on it.
**Muriel** (*huffily*) Yes, all right.
**Nip** (*to Father Molloy*) She's gorra lovely bum though.

*Father Molloy just manages to raise himself from a stupor and then sinks back*

**Mark** My wife and I would first of all like to thank you all for coming to this day's happening.
**Kevin** That's all right.
**Mark** To have you here has added to the happiness of today for both of us. My wife and myself and, of course, everybody here. (*He starts to flounder*) It has added tremendously . . . (*He tails off*)
**Harry** Hear, hear.

*There is an embarrassed silence*

**Muriel** (*in a loud whisper*) You thank the bridesmaids.
**Mark** I've got the wrong bit of paper. This is a receipt from Moss Bros.
**Father Molloy** (*banging the table*) Hear, hear, hear, hear.
**Mark** (*reddening*) Well, yes, so, ladies and gentlemen, I'll not keep you long.
**Nip** Bloody good job.
**Edith** Father, be quiet.
**Mark** So I'll just say: thank you, girls. (*He sits down*)
**Deirdre** You have to propose a toast.
**Mark** (*still sitting down*) Oh . . . Cheers.
**Muriel** (*in a loud whisper*) Stand up and toast the bridesmaids.
**Mark** (*shot to pieces*) Ladies and gentlemen—(*he stands up*)—the brides-maids.

*He sits down quickly leaving people standing up and sitting down in confusion muttering "The bridesmaids". When everyone has sat down again, Father Molloy, who didn't get up before, stands up*

**Father Molloy** Alla gansays good luck.

*Everybody looks round, puzzled*

**Hamish** I now call on the bride's father to make a speech—the bride's father.

*Everyone claps and bangs on the table*

**Nip** Go on Harry, make 'em 'ave it.

*Harry stands up and Father Molloy sits down*

**Harry** (*taking a piece of paper from his pocket*) Well, first I would like to thank you all for your good wishes to my wife and myself. (*He realizes he has got the groom's speech, gives it to him, and gets his own out of his hat*) Ladies and gentlemen, it's nice to know that at a time like this when England seems to be going to the dogs——

**Deirdre** Ooh, don't mention dogs!

**Harry** —that some people still believe that marriage and the family is still the basis of a strong society. (*He reads all the following very ponderously from a sheet of paper, having obviously copied it from something like the National Front Manifesto*) At a time when our womenfolk cannot walk the streets at night alone and when our institutions are mocked by Marxist Trotskyites and left-wing homosexuals it is nice to see Deirdre and Mark upholding true values. Oswald Mosley once said that a Greater Britain would only come through discipline and I know that Deirdre and Mark will uphold that too. On a higher note, I must tell you about a man who was arguing with his wife. A married couple they were. "Look at the dog and cat sleeping on the rug together," she said, "they're not fighting". "Yes, but tie their tails together and see what happens," said her husband.

*He pauses but there is no laughter. Ronald says "Hear hear" out of embarrassment, and people smile, perplexed, except Peter who by now has joined Nip and the priest in the race for oblivion. They are draining glasses at the rate of knots*

So it just remains for me to ask you to raise your glasses. I give you a Greater Britain with Deirdre and Mark. Deirdre and Mark.

*People stand and mumble and look confused except the three in the race for oblivion*

**Peter** Meirdre and Dark.

*As everyone sits down, Father Molloy stands up*

**Father Molloy** (*breathing heavily through his nose*) Laze chenman, the sacrament of marriage if a thing Sain Paul has concerned with wan he said "Take a little woman for your stomag's sake", now not being a married man meself—(*he laughs and goes to lean on the table but puts his hand in the sherry trifle*)—all I can say is tham talkin' of course merely from conjecture and text books, but it's a great thing for the church and may they both be happy and give you all my blessing. (*He raises his hand to bless them and showers them with trifle then sits down to an embarrassed silence*)

**Mark** What happens next?

**Muriel** Well, at all normal weddings, they cut the cake, then we go through for coffee while they clear up.

**Edith** Yes, come on everybody, let's cut the cake.

*The guests, apart from Nip, Peter and Father Molloy gather round to watch the cake being cut*

**Father Molloy** Motheragond yer lookitde power of a mess I'm in.

**Peter** You'd best go and clean yourself up in the back room.

**Nip** What room?

**Peter** There's a room in there where they keep all the Masonic gear. Stick him in there.

**Nip** Go on, take your trousers off and clean them. Yerra right mess. (*He pushes Father Molloy off* L)

*Father Molloy exits*

*At the same time there is a knock off* R. *Peter goes off* R *and comes back with the blow-up doll and the chains*

**Nip** Where the 'ell did you get that?

**Peter** A bobby's just given it to me. Said it were makin' 'em nervous at the station.

**Nip** You'd best gerrit owt of the way or there'll be trouble. Give it 'ere. (*He grabs the doll and throws it off* L, *after Father Molloy*)

*The guests begin to mingle again*

**Edith** I would like to apologize for what has happened.

**Muriel** (*to Edith*) That's all right, Edith, and do call me Muriel. Ronald and I would simply love to have you and Harold over to Moortop View some evening for a meal. You know where we live, don't you?

**Edith** Oh yes. It's where we used to play when we were little girls. There were all fields then near Daisy Dell.

**Muriel** That's right. Ronald managed to get the land very cheap. He knew the farmer Old Frost, you know. Ronald built all the bungalows and then we built "Shangri-La" for ourselves right on the top.

**Edith** How lovely.

**Muriel** Yes, it's nice after all the hard work to feel that it's been rewarded.

**Edith** Mark was your only one then?

**Muriel** Yes, Ronald couldn't have any more after a firework went up his trouser leg at the Coronation Bonfire. He's perfectly well, you know, but he just can't be fertile again. He always laughs to me and says he lost it serving his Queen.

**Ronald** Now what are you two talking about then?

**Edith** We were just talking about redundancy.

**Ronald** Well things are a little slack at present.

**Peter** (*coming up*) I thought you were doing well in the car trade.

**Ronald** Well, the car trade's doing well, but the taxi-ing is a bit down.

**Peter** Oh, I suppose they're expensive to run are they?

**Ronald** Well, moderately so . . .

*Deirdre and the bridesmaids come over*

**Deirdre** We're just going to get changed, Mother. We won't be long.
**Edith** All right, love. Can you manage?
**Deirdre** Oh, I'm sure we can. We'll hang the dresses up somewhere.

*Deirdre and the bridesmaids exit* L

**Peter** (*continuing the conversation, now quite drunk and pointing his fingers*)
I suppose the biggest expense is the fuel.
**Ronald** Well, that and the drivers' wages.

*Hamish and Mark come up*

**Hamish** Just going to slip out of the old Moss Bros. togs into something
a little less formal.
**Mark** Won't be long, Pop.
**Ronald** All right, son.

*Mark and Hamish exit* R

*Peter is pouring another glass down his throat, still talking at Ronald*

**Peter** But the fuel must be expensive?
**Ronald** Well it is expensive, yes.
**Peter** Very expensive.
**Ronald** I suppose so.
**Peter** Very, very expensive.
**Ronald** What the bloody hell are you getting at?
**Peter** All right mate, all right. I'll tell you——
**Edith** (*coming up*) Peter!
**Peter** Shut up, Mam. Right, I'll tell you. I write under the *nom de plume*
"Ned Ludd" of the *Grimesdale Alternative Free Press and Bugle* and I
know all about stinking Councillor Greenhalgh and the Corporation
Diesel.
**Ronald** So you're the little git, are you?
**Kevin**⎱
**Peter**⎰ (*singing together*) Ronald has only got one ball . . .
**Muriel** You're scum, you are. Scum spreading malicious lies like that.
**Peter** Lies. I've got witnesses who'll swear that twenty-seven thousand
gallons of diesel 'ave gone missing into your tanks over the last ten
years.
**Ronald** It was a leak. The Customs and Excise found a leak.
**Peter** After you'd gorrem well pissed in the Con Club. You're rotten
through and through.
**Muriel** I knew our Mark should never 'ave married into this family.
They're common as muck with evil minds and filthy mouths.
**Edith** 'Oo are you talking to, you blown up dog's dinner. You came from
Cloughbottom same as all of us, Mrs 'Igh and Mighty.
**Muriel** (*screaming*) You're nothing the whole lot of you. Nothing. She
only married 'im for is money. You're nothing the lot of you.

**Nip** Ee, are we 'avin' a scrap? You always get a scrap at a good weddin'.

**Muriel** And you can shut up, you dirty old man.

**Nip** You didn't say that back of the Public Baths after that Christmas dance in nineteen forty-three did you? "Get going," you said. "There's an air raid on, live now we may be dead tomorrow."

**Muriel** Oh, my God, I don't know what you're talking about.

**Ronald** What the 'ell does 'e mean? By God, I'll break his bloody neck for 'im.

*There are several screams off* R *that freeze everyone in their tracks*

*Deirdre runs in, wearing her knickers and bra*

**Deirdre** Oh, Mother. Father Molloy's in there with a naked woman. He frightened me to death. 'Ee were rollin' around an' groanin' in the dark.

**Ronald** Mad, the lot of 'em, stark raving mad.

*Hamish and Mark run in, in Y-fronts and string vests*

**Mark** What the bloody 'ell's happening?

**Hamish** What's going on, is someone hurt?

*Father Molloy staggers in wearing ecclesiastical underwear and his dog collar, carrying the doll and chains. He has some sort of Masonic headgear on*

**Edith** Holy Mother of God!

**Father Molloy** S'not mine at all. S'not mine at all. It belongs to him.

*He pushes it into Mark's arms and throws the chains round him*

**Muriel** What do you mean his? Mark is that—that thing yours?

**Mark** Well . . . well . . . I suppose so, at least the police——

**Muriel** My God the police!

**Ronald** I'll be bloody ruined!

**Nip** The bobbies brought it back. They caught him with it.

**Deirdre** What was he doing with it?

**Nip** He war practisin'.

**Deirdre** Oh Mother.

**Edith** Oh, my God. He's a pervert!

**Harry** A bloody rubber-doll fetishist—Hitler would have burnt 'im, bloody doll an' all.

*The Doll starts talking*

**Doll's Voice** Ooh! You are a big boy, ooh you are a big boy.

*The Doll starts to deflate and at that moment a row breaks out. Music plays over the chaos, with the action stopping and starting as flash bulbs go off, and—*

the CURTAIN *falls*

# FURNITURE AND PROPERTY LIST

## ACT I

Scene 1: The Ollerenshawes' living-room

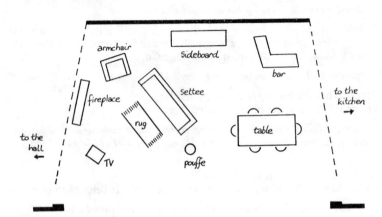

On stage·   Settee. *On it:* cushions, newspaper
           Armchair
           Fireplace with electric coal-effect fire (dressing). *On mantelpiece:*
               packet of cigarettes, box of matches, ashtray, various brass
               ornaments
           Pouffe
           Dining-table. *On it:* vase of plastic flowers
           6 chairs
           Sideboard. *On it:* photographs, including a large one of the Pope,
               radio, telephone, telephone directory
           Bar. *On it:* glasses, bottles of whisky, brandy etc., soda syphon
               covered with knitted poodle. *On wall behind it:* bullfight posters,
               plastic onions, straw-covered bottles
           Television. *On it:* packet containing copy of *Motor-cycle News*
           *On walls:* picture of the Queen, picture of the Sacred Heart with an
               electric candle (practical) beneath it
           Carpet
           Rug

Off stage:  Shopping bag containing packet of hamburgers, packet of cod pieces,
               2 tins of potatoes, tin of sweetcorn (**Edith**)
           Mug of tea (**Edith**)
           Mug of tea (**Edith**)

Tray with 6 knives, 6 forks, cruet set, bottle HP sauce, mugs, sugar-
    bowl, milk-jug, table-cloth (**Edith**)
Mug of tea (**Deirdre**)
Mug of tea (**Edith**)
Tray with 5 plates of cod pieces, potatoes and sweetcorn (**Edith**)
Pot of tea (**Nip**)
Shoe (**Peter**)
Plate of cod pieces, potatoes and sweetcorn (**Edith**)
Tray with 4 dishes of jam roly-poly and custard (**Edith**)
2 dishes of jam roly-poly and custard (**Deirdre**)

*Personal:*   *Note: these cover the whole play*
              **Father Molloy:** spectacles
              **Nip:** pipe, tobacco, matches

SCENES 2–5

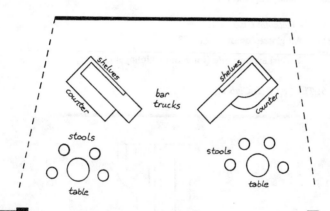

For these four scenes, two pub areas are set at either side of the stage, and the
scenes alternate between them. The basic items are as follows:

*On stage:*   2 bars mounted on stage trucks. *On counters:* ashtrays. *On shelves:*
              glasses, bottles of drink
              2 bar tables. *On them:* ashtrays
              8 low stools (4 round each table)

Props for the individual scenes are given below:

SCENE 2: *The Oddfellows* Tap Room
*Set:*        Glass and bottle of beer on counter (for **Nip**)
              2 trays, each with 3 pints bitter, 1 rum and lemonade, behind bar (for
              **Barmaid**)

*Off stage:*  dishcloth (**Barmaid**)

*Personal:*   *Note: these cover the rest of the act*
              **Nip:** money in pocket (including 3 coins for SCENE 3)

Hamish: money in pocket
Mark: money in pocket

SCENE 3: *The Friendship*

*Set:*        Half-full pint of bitter on counter (for **Harry**)
              Tray with 3 whiskies, 1 rum and lemonade, behind bar (for **Barmaid**)

*Personal:*   **Harry**: money in pocket (including £10 note for SCENE 6)

SCENE 4: *The Steam Shovel*

*Strike:*     All glasses used in SCENE 2

*Set:*        2 half-full pints of bitter on table (for **Peter** and **Jimmy**)
              Tray with 3 whiskies, 1 rum and lemonade, behind bar (for **Barmaid**)

*Personal:*   **Jimmy**: lighted joint

SCENE 5: *The Catholic Club*

*Strike:*     All glasses used in SCENE 3

*Set:*        2 whiskies on table (for **Father Molloy** and **Man**)

SCENE 6: *The Can Can Club*

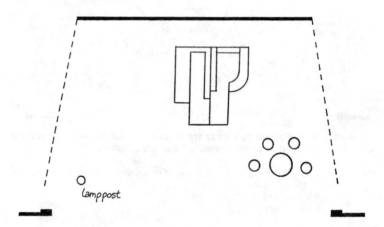

*Strike:*     1 bar table
              4 stools
              All glasses used in SCENES 4 and 5

*Set:*        2 bar trucks together
              Tray with 5 whiskies, 1 rum and lemonade, behind bar (for **Waiter**)
              Lamppost DR

*Off stage:*  Whip (**Evette**)
              Blown-up rubber doll in chains (**Stage Management**)

## ACT II

SCENE 1: The Ollerenshawes' living-room

*Strike:*    Any remaining items from table
             Deirdre's decorated coat and hat

*Set:*       Full packet of cigarettes on mantelpiece
             Whisky bottle back on bar
             Nip's jacket and shoes by settee
             Mug of tea by settee (for Nip)
             Turn pictures right way round

*Off stage:* Mug of tea (Peter)
             2 boxes of flowers (3 bouquets and 4 buttonholes) (Harry)
             Gun (Harry)
             Shopping bag containing black negligé with briefs, packet of tights
                 (Deirdre)
             Shopping bag containing purse with piece of paper in it (Edith)
             Mug of tea (Peter)
             Top hat (Nip)
             Tin of scouring powder (Peter)
             Pin (Edith)

SCENE 2: The Church

*On stage:*  Altar
             Pews set in two rows

*Personal:*  **Deirdre:** bouquet
             **Wendy:** bouquet
             **Kirstene:** bouquet
             **Hamish:** ring in pocket

SCENE 3: The Reception

*On stage:*  3 long tables. *On them:* tray with glasses of sherry, table-cloths,
             cutlery, plates of food, glasses, bottles of drink including wine and
             brandy, large bowl of trifle, wedding cake, large knife, telegrams
             for **Hamish**

*Off stage:* Blown-up rubber doll (Peter)
             Masonic headgear (Father Molloy)

*Personal:*  Mark: piece of paper in pocket
             Harry: piece of paper in pocket

# LIGHTING PLOT

Practical fittings required: pendant, flickering electric candle, TV
Property fittings required: electric coal-effect fire
One exterior and various interior settings

ACT I, Scene 1    Early evening
*To open:* Dim interior lighting

| | | |
|---|---|---|
| *Cue* 1 | **Edith** enters and switches on main light<br>*Snap on pendant and electric candle under Sacred Heart* | (Page 1) |
| *Cue* 2 | **Edith** moves downstage to address the audience<br>*Fade to spot on* **Edith** | (Page 2) |
| *Cue* 3 | **Edith:** ". . . life goes on, dun't it?"<br>*Return to previous lighting* | (Page 2) |
| *Cue* 4 | **Kevin** enters DR<br>*Fade to spot on* **Kevin** | (Page 2) |
| *Cue* 5 | **Kevin:** ". . . and I quite liked it."<br>*Return to previous lighting* | (Page 3) |
| *Cue* 6 | **Kevin** switches on TV<br>*Snap on TV effect* | (Page 3) |
| *Cue* 7 | **Deirdre** enters DR<br>*Fade to spot on* **Deirdre** | (Page 3) |
| *Cue* 8 | **Deirdre:** ". . . I hated PE at school."<br>*Return to previous lighting* | (Page 3) |
| *Cue* 9 | **Nip** enters DR<br>*Fade to spot on* **Nip** | (Page 6) |
| *Cue* 10 | **Nip:** ". . . over twenty-one anyway."<br>*Return to previous lighting* | (Page 6) |
| *Cue* 11 | **Harry** moves downstage<br>*Fade to spot on* **Harry** | (Page 7) |
| *Cue* 12 | **Harry:** ". . . to run consecutively."<br>*Return to previous lighting* | (Page 7) |
| *Cue* 13 | **Peter** enters DR<br>*Fade to spot on* **Peter** | (Page 9) |
| *Cue* 14 | **Peter:** "I pinch most of me ideas."<br>*Return to previous lighting* | (Page 10) |
| *Cue* 15 | **Mark** enters DR<br>*Fade to spot on* **Mark** | (Page 11) |

| *Cue* 33 | **Ronald:** ". . . and our gratuities." | (Page 38) |
| | *Fade to spot on* **Ronald** | |
| *Cue* 34 | **Ronald:** ". . . well at nights." | (Page 38) |
| | *Return to previous lighting* | |
| *Cue* 35 | Doll starts to deflate and row breaks out | (Page 45) |
| | *Flashes—continue until* CURTAIN *falls* | |

# EFFECTS PLOT

## ACT I

*Cue* 1    **Edith** switches on radio              (Page 1)
*Snap on radio broadcast—DJ's voice and music*

*Cue* 2    **Edith** switches off radio             (Page 2)
*Snap off radio broadcast*

*Cue* 3    **Kevin** switches on TV               (Page 3)
*Snap on TV sound—introductory music to children's
    programme*

*Cue* 4    **Edith:** "Our Kevin!!!" (*She takes another fag*)    (Page 5)
*Door slam, off*

*Cue* 5    **Edith:** ". . . like a load of animals."        (Page 12)
*Knock on door, off*

*Cue* 6    **Father Molloy:** ". . . light on in the snug!"    (Page 13)
*Irish jig music to cover scene change—fade when ready*

*Cue* 7    **Nip:** ". . . a drink last year."            (Page 16)
*Build background pub noises; fade slightly as* **Harry** *begins
    speaking*

*Cue* 8    **Harry:** ". . . senile like that."           (Page 17)
*Build background pub noises and music; fade slightly as*
    **Peter** *begins speaking*

*Cue* 9    **Nip:** ". . . splash of lemonade."         (Page 19)
*Build background noises and music; fade slightly as* **Father**
    **Molloy** *begins speaking*

*Cue* 10   **Nip:** ". . . large rum an' lemonade."      (Page 20)
*Build heavy rock music; fade slightly as the gang sit down*

*Cue* 11   **Bouncer:** ". . . the lovely Evette."       (Page 21)
*Stripping music*

*Cue* 12   **Father Molloy:** ". . . knocked off me bike."   (Page 22)
*Stop stripping music abruptly*

*Cue* 13   **Mark** (*singing*): "I'm getting married in the morning . . ." (Page 23)
*Start tape of Doll's voice*

## ACT II

*Cue* 14   **Kevin:** ". . . they got away anyway."     (Page 26)
*Dustbins knocked over, something dropping, a shot and a
    dog howling, all off*

*Cue* 15   **Deirdre, Kirstene** and **Wendy** exit      (Page 31)
*Church bells pealing and organ music*

*Cue* 16    **Muriel** blows a kiss to **Mark** and dabs her eyes                (Page 32)
            *Fade organ music*

*Cue* 17    **Muriel:** "But who's counting?"                                    (Page 32)
            *Organ music, swelling then dying gradually*

*Cue* 18    **Father Molloy** enters                                             (Page 33)
            *Organ music "Here Comes the Bride"; as **Deirdre** and **Mark**
              reach altar, fade into background hymn music*

*Cue* 19    **Nip:** ". . . in there or what?"                                   (Page 34)
            *Organ music: "The Wedding March"*

*Cue* 20    As Lights come up on the Reception                                   (Page 35)
            *Fade organ music*

*Cue* 21    **Father Molloy** exits L                                            (Page 43)
            *Knock off* R

*Cue* 22    **Harry:** ". . . bloody doll an' all."                              (Page 45)
            *Start tape of Doll's voice*

*Cue* 23    Row breaks out                                                       (Page 45)
            *Music plays over chaos; continue until* CURTAIN *falls*

MADE AND PRINTED IN GREAT BRITAIN BY
LATIMER TREND & COMPANY LTD PLYMOUTH
MADE IN ENGLAND